The Advantage of Lyric

The Advantage of Lyric

Essays on Feeling in Poetry

BARBARA HARDY

INDIANA UNIVERSITY PRESS

Bloomington and London

Manufactured in Great Britain

Library of Congress catalog card number: 76-47167
ISBN 0-253-30130-0

For Martin Dodsworth

Acknowledgments

I am very grateful for the help of the following friends and colleagues: Martin Dodsworth, James Britton, Nancy Martin and Jean Elliott.

Chapter One draws on material used in a lecture given to the London Association for the Teaching of English, subsequently published in the N.A.T.E. Bulletin *Poetry*, vol. iii, no. 1, Spring 1966. Chapter Two was first published in *John Donne: Essays in Celebration*, ed. A. J. Smith, Methuen and Co. Ltd, London, 1972; Chapter Three in *The Major Victorian Poets: Reconsiderations*, Routledge and Kegan Paul, London, 1969; Chapter Four is a slightly abridged version of the First Annual Lecture of the Hopkins Society given on the 12 February 1970 and subsequently printed by the Society; Chapter Five was first published in *Modernist Studies*, vol. i, no. 2, 1974; Chapter Six in *The Review*, no. 11/12, 1964; Chapter Seven in *The Southern Review*, vol. v, new series, no. 3, July 1969; Chapter Eight in *Poetry Wales*, vol. ix, no. 2, Autumn 1973; and Chapter Nine in *The Survival of Poetry*, ed. Martin Dodsworth, Faber and Faber, London, 1970. I am grateful to the editors and publishers for their permission to reprint. The reprinted essays have been corrected and slightly revised but not updated in references.

B.H.

Contents

I

The Advantage of Lyric

Lyric poetry isolates feeling in small compass and so renders it at its most intense. To say more about the form is to raise doubts and exceptions. The advantage of lyric to the critic is its easy access, which permits inspection of its form in a way not often feasible in longer works.

But the advantage of lyric in itself is its concentrated and patterned expression of feeling. This advantage is negatively definable: the lyric does not provide an explanation, judgment or narrative; what it does provide is feeling, alone and without histories or characters. A good example is a sonnet of Shakespeare's:

> To me, fair friend, you never can be old,
> For as you were when first your eye I ey'd,
> Such seems your beauty still. Three winters cold
> Have from the forests shook three summers' pride,
> Three beauteous springs to yellow autumn turn'd
> In process of the seasons have I seen,
> Three April perfumes in three hot Junes burn'd,
> Since first I saw you fresh, which yet are green.
> Ah! yet doth beauty, like a dial-hand,
> Steal from his figure, and no pace perceiv'd;
> So your sweet hue, which methinks still doth stand,
> Hath motion, and mine eye may be deceiv'd:
>   For fear of which, hear this, thou age unbred:
>   Ere you were born was beauty's summer dead.

To call this sonnet an expression of feeling may seem tendentious, when in fact it contains ideas, subjects or themes: time, nature's renewal, human beauty. These subjects are admittedly present, but they are marshalled in the service of feeling. Love is dramatised, expressed in a way that informs the poem with qualities that belong to love: warmth, exhilaration, cool appraisal and then hotblooded praise. The poem is typical of lyric poetry in that it creates and discovers feeling under the guise of affirming it, and does not have to discuss, analyse, explain or imitate it. So the structure of the poem is not merely an adherence to a sonnet scheme, but an image of the poet's thought as it moves, grows tense, and gathers into itself the unity and variety directly expressive of love.

The advantage of lyric poetry comes from its undiluted attention to feeling and feeling alone, and its articulateness in clarifying that feeling, in attesting conviction or what may somewhat misleadingly be called sincerity, and transferring this from privacy to publicity. What is expressed here is feeling; time and beauty, as they are contemplated, only go to enhance that feeling. The rumination is only pseudo-philosophical, as if time and beauty could claim only a limited degree of pertinence to the main subject. If the poem is said to be about beauty, one can see why, yet beauty is not expressed as in a painting by Velasquez. The poem is about time, in the same way, yet does not express duration or ageing as Proust takes time to do; these are instruments by which the central feeling can be registered. This sonnet is a true instance of Coleridge's definition of poetry as 'A more than usual state of emotion, with more than usual order'.

Lyric poetry thrives, then, on exclusions. It is more than usually opaque because it leaves out so much of the accustomed context and consequences of feeling that it can speak in a pure, lucid, and intense voice. The voice of lyric usually manages to speak only in private relationships or solitude where it relies on more or less than words; but when it makes itself heard publicly, it is presenting an element, ordinarily known only in compounds, in isolated splendour.

In the Shakespeare sonnet just quoted, the feeling is complex and dynamic, flowing changingly but continuously through the imagery and address. The poem's beginning expresses the almost unnecessary reassurances of love, natural, expected, said warmly, quietly and simply: 'To me, fair friend, you never can be old'. This moves into the more exhilarating tone of the delicate punning (very like the later passionate speeches of Juliet) in 'when first your eye I ey'd' which has a playfulness one can only describe as *fond*. In the next part of the poem, which carries feeling through a description of seasonal rhythm, there are strongly placed words belonging to a fluid world of metaphor and common feeling: 'cold', 'pride', 'beauteous', 'yellow', 'perfumes' and 'hot' can all belong to the world of man as well as to the world of nature. They appear after the establishment of personal feeling, so that nature is summoned as witness into the lovers' circle. But the poet comes back to the purely human feeling and validates these open metaphors with the sentence which relates back in image and antithesis: 'Since first I saw you fresh, which yet are green'. The note of sadness comes in, though it is restrained and conveyed in tones of reluctant but necessary rational admission. As he expands the context to admit nature and then time as onlookers, the lover has to allow them some independent power, and in so doing, to acknowledge the possibility of love's blindness, in the enlarged context in which he comes to contemplate love and human beauty: 'Ah! yet doth beauty, like a dial-hand,' he sighs, but mutedly, and 'So your sweet hue . . .' he adores while he insists on necessity: 'Hath motion, and mine eye may be deceiv'd'. These lines have that indefinable note, neither wry nor dry, which so often puts an edge on praise and longing in Shakespeare's sonnets. Shakespeare, like Donne, manages superbly to find a language for love which, allowing reflection, subordinates it to passion.

Although lyric poetry is not discursive, it is capable of speaking its feelings intelligently, so as to speak about them. The double voice of feeling can speak in a single form, as it must, fusing reflection or even analysis with the stirring passion. Just as we are often aware of feeling while possessed by it so the lyric poet can speak a commentary on his feeling which neither chills nor distances. Sometimes this implicitly evaluates the state of feeling, as in some of Shakespeare's most bitter sonnets, where the prevailing feeling appears to blend desire and disgust, reproach and pride, grief and elation. When one reads the sonnets as a whole in sequence, there emerges a shadowy story, with characters and events, so that the individual lyrics are both intense expressions of moments of feeling, and also imply a buried narrative. It is a submerged and suggested story whose action and relationships are often dark, and the frustrations of critics who find it hard to tolerate imperfect knowledge simply emphasise the lyric poet's high-handed way with narrative. All we are certain of is the feeling, not the characters and conditions. Allusion replaces the detailed specifications of drama and fiction, whose business is telling as much as possible.

We can of course find intensities in novels. One of the many imaginative virtues of Beckett's novels, for instance, is their capacity to express unformulated feeling, and his dislocations and fluidities of event, point of view and character, seem to forgo some of the advantages of prose fiction and aspire to the condition of poetry. Less shifty

writers can also use foreshortening, though it may expose their work
to the kind of speculation they seem to want to thwart. At the end of
Ulysses, Joyce emphasises the coming-together of Stephen Dedalus and
Leopold Bloom. Their feelings, expressed and covert, cold and warm,
are conveyed, but their future history forms no part of the novel,
except in the inventive conjectures of readers who, while shunning
inquiry into the later adventures of swearers of eternal love, would,
nevertheless, carry on this narrative beyond the author's conclusion.

Emily Brontë suffers from the same kind of inappropriate conjecture.
She expresses feeling by the drastic excision of explanations and histories. Her poetry is an excellent introduction to her novel because it so
obviously and effectively refuses to tell. In the short poem 'Spellbound',
for instance, the structure of feeling depends on our total ignorance of
causes. The feeling is bared, to move us, as it moves towards a spell-
binding assertion of bondage, denying a knowledge of causes:

> The night is darkening round me,
> The wild winds coldly blow;
> But a tyrant spell has bound me
> And I cannot, cannot go.
>
> The Giant trees are bending
> Their bare boughs weighed with snow,
> And the storm is fast descending
> And yet I cannot go.
>
> Clouds beyond clouds above me,
> Wastes beyond wastes below;
> But nothing drear can move me;
> I will not, cannot go.

Emily Brontë, in her way, is capable of challenging our limited
vocabulary of feeling, by evoking feelings without histories. The names,
if she does name, might be ascribed to angels or devils as well as men.
In 'Remembrance' the speaker names one state of feeling after another:
'Change and suffering', 'Sterner desires and darker hopes', 'tears of
useless passion', 'Memory's rapturous pain', 'divinest anguish'. Yet none
of these namings can fix the complex feeling formed in the course of
the poem—a feeling for a remembered feeling, a recognition that to

live on is to outlast even dear feelings, a tender urge to explain, persuade
and argue the sense and value of that transformation of passion which
is discovered in the act of the poem.

Often, however, Emily Brontë's poems are less sustained, and the
lyrical impulse is burdened with details of Gondal history which seem
alien to her poetic talent. As a result some of her poems are improved
by cutting and selection. For instance, the long poem 'Julian M. and
A. G. Rochelle' was published in a shortened (and slightly altered)
version in *Poems by Currer, Ellis and Acton Bell* in 1846 under the title
'The Prisoner. A Fragment'. It has since been cut down still more in
numerous anthologies (Arthur Quiller-Couch's 1921 edition of *The
Oxford Book of English Verse* for example) until virtually all we are left
with is the intense lyrical evocation of Hope:

> Still let my tyrants know, I am not doom'd to wear
> Year after year in gloom and desolate despair;
> A messenger of Hope comes every night to me,
> And offers for short life, eternal liberty.
>
> He comes with western winds, with evening's wandering airs,
> With that clear dusk of heaven that brings the thickest stars;
> Winds take a pensive tone, and stars a tender fire,
> And visions rise and change which kill me with desire—
>
> Desire for nothing known in my maturer years
> When joy grew mad with awe at counting future tears;
> When, if my spirit's sky was full of flashes warm,
> I knew not whence they came, from sun or thunderstorm;
>
> But first a hush of peace, a soundless calm descends;
> The struggle of distress and fierce impatience ends;
> Mute music soothes my breast—unuttered harmony
> That I could never dream till earth was lost to me.
>
> Then dawns the Invisible, the Unseen its truth reveals;
> My outward sense is gone, my inward essence feels—
> Its wings are almost free, its home its harbour found;
> Measuring the gulf it stoops and dares the final bound!

Oh, dreadful is the check—intense the agony
When the ear begins to hear and the eye begins to see;
When the pulse begins to throb, the brain to think again,
The soul to feel the flesh and the flesh to feel the chain!

Yet I would lose no sting, would wish no torture less;
The more that anguish racks the earlier it will bless;
And robed in fires of Hell, or bright with heavenly shine,
If it but herald Death, the vision is divine.

When we put it back into its full narrative context, however, it turns out to be a very different poem. It is no longer metaphysical, an image of spirit tormented by flesh, but a literal description of physical imprisonment. With the arrival of the hero Julian, and the glimpse of rescue, the reckless divine or diabolical vision is rejected: 'Earth's hope was not so dead, heaven's home was not so drear'.

Novelists are occasionally jealous of the intensity of lyric poetry, and seek in one way or another to incorporate it into their larger schemes. But they are sometimes aware of the limitations of lyrical declaration. The Victorian novelist usually aspires to give full explanations of the affective life and cannot isolate the passions. Emily Brontë foreshortens the presentation of Heathcliff's desires and torments, but still records them with some sense of causality. George Eliot, a much less lyrical genius, in her poetry as well as in her novels, places the intensities of her characters in a full historical context. In *Middlemarch* we move on from Dorothea Brooke's several episodes of antagonistic and destructive feeling, which is momentarily given its head, to her rational appraisal and judgment. If George Eliot were a lyric poet she could express the impassioned distaste, or tenderness of vision, in isolation, well aware that human beings revise and review their torments and bliss. On one occasion in *Middlemarch* she implicitly compares the cut-off lyric with the full prose narrative, performing the rare feat of inserting an actual lyric into the novel. It is the lyric composed by Will Ladislaw as he walks through the fields one sunny morning, putting into words and music his feelings for Dorothea whom he is looking forward to seeing in Lowick Church. The poem, not distinguished, but not a bad one, takes its emotional colour from hope, tenderness, expectation, sunlight, movement. It also expresses the experience of being content and enjoying the contentment in a double voice which feels and desires to sustain the feeling. But since Will's feeling of love is an adulterous one, for all its sprightly innocence, the complacency of its self-contentment cannot be allowed to live unchecked. Will puts into his song a feeling of willing renunciation:

> O me, O me, what frugal cheer
>   My love doth feed upon!
> A touch, a ray, that is not here,
>   A shadow that is gone:
>
> A dream of breath that might be near,
>   An inly-echoed tone,
> The thought that one may think me dear,
>   The place where one was known,
>
> The tremor of a banished fear,
>   An ill that was not done—
> O me, O me, what frugal cheer
>   My love doth feed upon!   (ch. 47)

There is something morally flattering about the experience of this fragile mood and George Eliot is too Rhadamanthine to permit such indulgence. Will has to find out that what is actually involved is much more frugal than the cheer he has been putting into those happily expectant words and measures. George Eliot does not pass her judgment explicitly. The composition of the poem is carefully timed, coming after Will's conscientious debate which ends with the defeat of 'Objection by force of unreason'. It is carefully placed, on the walk across a common and past a wood, 'as if he had been on the way to Paradise'. The irony is delicate: George Eliot does not subject Will to harsh criticism, but as she bestows on him a lyrical eloquence she makes plain the fragility of the medium. Actual deprivation is less nourishing, as the story comes to show.

In *A Portrait of the Artist as a Young Man* Joyce uses poetry in a somewhat similar way, making Stephen Dedalus write two poems to characterise his youth as a poet and to indicate failure and fruition. One poem is a fragment of bad poetry, coming in one of Stephen's spells of moroseness, when the world around turns dead, and the deadness is extended to language and signs. Like George Eliot, Joyce carefully times and places the writing of the poem. Stephen is retreating from the thought of his friend Cranly's 'dark womanish eyes', and also from his own listlessness. Inhibition leads to a perverted poetic action:

Through this image he had a glimpse of a strange dark cavern of speculation but at once turned away from it, feeling that it was not yet the hour to enter it. But the nightshade of his friend's listlessness seemed to be diffusing in the air around him a tenuous and deadly exhalation; and he found himself glancing from one casual word to another on his right or left in stolid wonder that they had been so silently emptied of instantaneous sense until every mean shop legend bound his mind like the words of a spell and his soul shrivelled up sighing with age as he walked on in a lane among heaps of dead language. His own consciousness of language was ebbing from his brain and trickling into the very words themselves which set to band and disband themselves in wayward rhythms:

> The ivy whines upon the wall,
> And whines and twines upon the wall,
> The yellow ivy upon the wall,
> Ivy, ivy up the wall.

Did any one ever hear such drivel? Lord Almighty! Who ever heard of ivy whining on a wall? Yellow ivy: that was all right. Yellow ivory also. And what about ivory ivy?

The word now shone in his brain, clearer and brighter than any ivory sawn from the mottled tusks of elephants. *Ivory, ivoire, avario, ebur.*   (pt. 5)

In the act of composition he moves back into the sense of the vitality of the word. The drivelling verses are still verses, for Joyce knows that going through the motions and measures of composition can revive the action of mind and feelings.

On the second occasion in the novel when we see Stephen composing poetry, the inspiration seems to be a sexual dream.[1] The poem is composed quickly, and written down on a piece of a cigarette packet. Joyce lets the poem gather together and transmute—his metaphor is transubstantiate—the events and words of the previous day. What gets into the poem is development of feeling, and the facts, even of previous

---

[1] For a fuller discussion of this episode in a different context, see my *Tellers and Listeners: The Narrative Imagination* (London, 1975), pp. 243–5.

feeling, are considerably changed. The composition is an active demonstration that the feeling of poetry exists in the poem, and does not stand
in a passive relation to words and structures; it is more than mere
material. Stephen has felt an enchantment of the heart in his dream.
That enchantment fires the writing of the poem, but gets into it
negatively, 'Tell no more of enchanted days'. Joyce shows Stephen
remembering, in the elaborate narrative form of memory, the episodes
with E.C., but the recorded jealousy and hostility to her flirtation with
the priest are not legible within the poem, having passed into admiration and pity for a larger seductiveness. The individual woman becomes
the *femme fatale*:

> *Our broken cries and mournful lays*
> *Rise in one eucharistic hymn.*
> *Are you not weary of ardent ways?*

> *While sacrificing hands upraise*
> *The chalice flowing to the brim,*
> *Tell no more of enchanted days.*

> *And still you hold our longing gaze*
> *With languorous look and lavish limb!*
> *Are you not weary of ardent ways?*
> *Tell no more of enchanted days.* (pt. 5)

Feelings are evoked and shaped, then worked up and worked out into
larger feelings. The result is a generalisation of character but a vivid
particularity of feeling, present, active, neither imitated nor revived.
The absence of history, character and analysis is made explicit by the
purposeful contrast between the medium of prose narrative, and the
medium of poetry. Like George Eliot, Joyce performs an intricate act
of dramatic demonstration which is locally effective and shows the
sense of using one genre within the other. When Joyce comes to make
his distinction between the three literary genres, lyric, epic and drama,
he is not exempt from the usual temptation of distinction-makers, and
greatly simplifies the definition of lyric in order to argue a progress
towards drama. His own development from indifferent lyric poetry
to the triumphs of his fiction suits this hierarchy. He describes lyrical
form as 'the simplest verbal gesture of an instant of emotion, a rhythmi-
cal cry such as ages ago cheered on the man who pulled at the oar or

dragged stones up a slope', but his dramatic portrayal of lyrical composition shows that he had more to say and illustrate on the subject.
It could be argued that Stephen's *villanelle* is Joyce's best lyric poem,
having more subject and more emotional pressure than those published
under his own name.

Joyce ignores the action of lyrical brooding when he describes the
lyrical speaker as 'more conscious of the instant of emotion than of
himself as feeling emotion'. In fact, Stephen shows a double consciousness, of the instant and the feeling self, as does Shakespeare. Even a
simple poem like Thomas Nashe's 'Spring' does much more than
simply express an instant of feeling. It prolongs it, and by prolonging
generates new feeling. One way of dwelling on feeling, as everyone
knows from the experiences of prolonging desire or bad temper, is
through putting feeling into words. By expressing feeling, the poet
retails and explores it, and so amplifies the feeling. In Nashe's poem,
the poet is engaged in gathering happy instances, like flowers:

> Spring, the sweet Spring, is the year's pleasant king;
> Then blooms each thing, then maids dance in a ring,
> Cold doth not sting, the pretty birds do sing,
>   Cuckoo, jug-jug, pu-we, to-witta-woo!
>
> The palm and may make country houses gay,
> Lambs frisk and play, the shepherds pipe all day,
> And we hear ay birds tune this merry lay,
>   Cuckoo, jug-jug, pu-we, to-witta-woo!
>
> The fields breathe sweet, the daisies kiss our feet,
> Young lovers meet, old wives a-sunning sit,
> In every street these tunes our ears do greet,
>   Cuckoo, jug-jug, pu-we, to-witta-woo!
>   Spring! the sweet Spring!

The emotion is fuelled by more than repetition; images of delight are
delightedly accumulated. In argument or passion, we may choose
illustrations or images which outstrip the original purpose. Hence the
surprise of currents of feeling or thought, inside or outside poetry. In a
poem, the metrical exigencies play an important part in generating
new material, for they insist on certain arbitrary choices and patterns.
Nashe's scheme of internal rhyme probably produced the sudden

arrival of the negative instance in the middle of the positives, 'Cold doth not sting'. The onomatopoeic refrain also introduces a stylised pressure; each verse must get round, or get back, to the birdsong. It also has a sub-verbal effect, like that of lovers' or parents' brooding murmurs. But even this simple poem shows a characteristic effort of growth. The first two verses do little more than accrete images and keep the feeling alive in a perfectly valid and delightful exercise, but the last verse starts stretching and developing the examples. The illustrations begin to join up and connect, the fields' sweet breath moving into the precise and unmetaphorical daisies which then move back again into the metaphor of the kiss. Young lovers are poised against old wives. By particularisation and antithesis, the list becomes more shapely than a list, and in the final verse the simple repetition of the refrain itself is not sufficient for a climax, but has to be capped by the salute, 'Spring! the sweet Spring!' The poem does more than return to the beginning and appeals finally in an extra line, exuberant in an exclamation which has gone a long way beyond the quiet indicative of the beginning.

Delight, even in such a simply presented poem, is mixed with the conscious brooding on delight. As it lists and shapes pleasures, the poem also reflects on them: 'Spring, the sweet Spring, is the year's pleasant king'. The adjectives 'pretty', 'merry', 'sweet', insist that the feeling of delight is a delightful possession. The poem contains its own motive, and reveals its own mainspring.

Reflection of this kind, itself part of the affective experience inside and outside poetry, is not discussion. The lyric offers little or no place for anything not incorporable into an emotional state. Writers who are concerned to analyse feeling write novels like Proust's; those who are concerned to judge feeling write novels like George Eliot's. Those who are concerned to name and understand the growth and variety of feeling use literary forms which give scope for history, psychology, and sociology. The poet primarily concerned with elucidating and particularising individual feelings writes lyric. Our need for this kind of lucid and intense expression of feeling need not be laboured. We have insufficient time and scope for feeling, surrounded as we are by all the business, and all the classifying, judging, and analysing apparatus, of an environment where even introverts have no time to be anything but extroverted. Coleridge spoke of the lubricating effect of music, and we can extend his precise metaphor to the effects of lyric poetry.

If a more ethical or educational metaphor seemed necessary, we could propose catharsis; not the catharsis of tragedy in which pity and fear are summoned and dispelled, but a lyric catharsis in which private or secret feelings are released in public vestments. Lyric poems often have the privacy of love-speech, but equally often the greater privacy of inner discourse. Reading and writing the poetry of feeling is plainly a valuable means of achieving what Proust speaks of as sentimental honesty. Some poetry has the melodramatic quality of attempts to stir feeling and sensation, but good poetry is not written out of this kind of imposed and strained (often well-meaning, but possibly dangerous) desire to *move*, but moves its readers by keeping its eye on the elucidation and development of feeling. This is not to expound a naturalistic doctrine: a love poem may or may not be written from actual feeling, but may assemble and imagine and create from the basis of real experience. Perhaps the best discussion of feeling in poetry written since Coleridge is the prose discourse, 'Dichtung Und Wahrheit' in Auden's *Homage to Clio*, where Auden insists on the subjunctive mood of poetic passion:

> As an artistic language, Speech has many advantages—three persons, three tenses (Music and Painting have only the Present Tense) both the active and the passive mood—but it has one serious defect: it lacks the Indicative Mood. All its statements are in the subjunctive and only possibly true until verified (which is not always possible) by non-verbal evidence.

There are many feelings which evaporate on being specified. Lyrical utterance makes feeling public, yet preserves a privacy in declining to furnish attendant circumstances. D. H. Lawrence speaks of the danger of pinning things down in fiction, of trying to make static what is trembling and irridescent. In Shakespeare's sonnet we follow the very track of feeling, moving through delicacy and strength, rational appraisal and irrational defiance at the end, sadness and exhilaration, gentleness and great pride, moth-like softness and a climax as passionate and affirmative as an embrace. In Robert Frost's poem 'Stopping by Woods on a Snowy Evening' the narrative glimpses have the function of shutting off history, and deepening the opacity. The poem would lose its fugitive resonance if we knew precisely what promises the poet had to keep. Poetry gains both specificity and generalising power from appearing out of context, and Frost's poem is sufficiently opaque and vague to let us identify a great number of things with his lovely, dark, and deep woods—death, beauty, desire, danger, freedom, wildness. Auden was an admirer of Frost's reticence and in many lyrics of Auden, both early and late, the sharpness of apprehensions comes from a similar ability to free us from history. The nightmare pressures of 'As I walked out one evening' can be confronted directly, like the desires in 'Stopping by Woods', their power and urgency undiminished by analysis. Lyric poetry preserves the ephemeral life of feeling where philosophical or narrative poetry would kill it by providing too much ballast. The best lyric poems express the individual quality of individual states of feeling and the absence of character and history is a positive strength and a symptom of the poet's concern, his truthfulness and his sense of proportion.

If lyric poetry can show how feeling shapes itself within individual affective experiences of fairly short duration, it can also show how feelings grow and change over longer periods of time. Verse-sequences, and the revisions of verse, illustrate most clearly the impossibility of repeating feeling. In a sequence of lyrical poems like Shakespeare's sonnets or D. H. Lawrence's 'The Ship of Death', mood and passion are prolonged, as of course they may often be outside poetry. A lyric poem may resemble an outburst of feeling, and a series of lyric poems, or a long poem with lyrical episodes, may resemble the sustained states of feeling we experience in the life we lead outside poems. As Lawrence so well knew, as he wrote of and wrote about the rhythm of our intensities, feeling may last, but is never static. No one moment or hour of feeling seems to resemble another. As Wordsworth declared, poetry often tries to recollect past emotion. Wordsworth was concerned with the attempt to recall emotion in states of tranquillity, but we may need to make the attempt from more turbulent moods. When Lawrence himself comes to revise his poems, the present feeling seems to take over the past. So the two versions of 'The Wild Common' and of 'Piano' (earlier called 'The Piano')[1] are strikingly different from each other, as if the process of revising form and language were also a process of clarifying and so revising feeling. The process of revision may even engender new feeling. In 'The Wild Common' the second attempt makes out of one experience another, which has enough similarity with it to be still expressible in some of the old words and forms. But the later version cuts out much emotional circumstance, reducing a

[1] The early drafts are printed in Appendix III of *The Complete Poems of D. H. Lawrence*, ed. Vivian de Sola Pinto and Warren Roberts (London, 1964).

diffuse eroticism to bring about a clearer and more urgent sensuality. Compare, for example,

> Oh but the water loves me and folds me,
> Plays with me, sways me, lifts me and sinks me as though it
>   were living blood,
> Blood of a heaving woman who holds me,
> Owning my supple body a rare glad thing, supremely good.

with the later version of the same stanza:

> Oh but the water loves me and folds me,
> Plays with me, sways me, lifts me and sinks me, murmurs: Oh
>   marvellous stuff!
> No longer shadow!—and it holds me
> Close, and it rolls me, enfolds me, touches me, as if never it
>   could touch me enough.

Lawrence said that his more youthful poetry often inhibited his demon, and the revisions he worked at frequently give that demon a louder and more lucid say. But the gain is not purely one of emotional intensity, for feeling is inseparable from argument. The second version establishes satisfactorily the belief in unity of substance and shadow, and shows the poet coming to understand what the first attempt failed not only to achieve but to see. This is true also of the revisions of 'Piano', which gives us, incidentally, an interesting example of Lawrence using the *same* word to express completely different emotions. In the first version he writes of the 'glamour' of the present music in contrast to the remembrance of his 'mother's tunes', but in the second, 'glamour' is used of the past—'The glamour of childish days is upon me'. The generation of feeling and knowledge of feeling takes the hand off the mouth of the demon. We can see the process which Lawrence called 'the welling-up of new life into consciousness' at work in the fresh contemplation of older forms of feeling. We can also see from such total transformations why Lawrence was incapable of doing patchwork revisions, in verse or prose.[1]

---

[1] Lawrence's revisions are, of course, not unique. Revision may often simplify and intensify the form of feeling through unloading biographical circumstance which seems indispensable at the time of first composition. The two versions of Coleridge's 'Dejection: An Ode' show the process plainly. In the original poem 'Letter to Sara Hutchinson', the poet includes details of his relationship with Sara

The welling-up of new emotions into consciousness can be seen in sequences of poems, which incorporate the act of emotional revision into the structure of poetry. Shakespeare's sonnets show that emotion cannot be repeated. As Shakespeare writes his variations on the theme of reproduction, persuading the young man to beget progeny, the argument gathers feeling. It moves from the form of argument for the preservation of blood and beauty, coloured by some affection, admiration, and occasional distaste, to the more personally urgent argument about defeating time, which in its turn generates the poet's feeling that his poetry will act as preservative and memorial. Feeling is part of an argument, warming, sustaining, and generating fresh poetic ideas. A poetic idea is a passionate idea, warming, sustaining, and generating fresh feeling.

Similarly, Lawrence's meditations on death in 'The Ship of Death' and the group of related poems, propagate new forms of feeling by brooding, repeating and varying words and images. The growth is slow: from preparations for dying to the dying, from oblivion to revival, from pain to death to peace, and then 'the whole thing starts again'. Lawrence's habit is to repeat words and phrases, not statically but with faint shifts of feeling. 'We are dying', 'gone', 'wait' and 'oblivion' are words which brood and change. Feeling is fluid and dynamic.

The same process of fluidity and growth appears even in his short poems. Lawrence's essays in free verse were made in the effort to get out the curve of emotion, purely and clearly. He writes strongly impassioned poetry, generally freer from what he called the didactic voice of the author than his prose versions of similar emotional states, especially feelings of submission and feelings of conjunction,[1] but his poetry makes brilliantly plain the process of passionate thinking. One of his shorter free-verse poems is not only concerned with the question

Hutchinson, judgments on his 'coarse domestic life' and a complete history of the emotions expressed in the poem. This version could not be made public, and the revised poem, 'Dejection: An Ode', shows not only a tactful reticence but a compression which makes the pattern of feeling strong and clear. Cause and effect are eliminated. We no longer know the origin of the poet's dulled response, or of his need for 'abstruse research', or of the nature of the 'viper thoughts' which he has to reject towards the end, but the gain in intensity more than offsets the loss in explanation.

[1] For a discussion of Lawrence's two *media* of feeling, see my essay, 'Women in D. H. Lawrence's Works', in *D. H. Lawrence: Novelist, Poet, Prophet*, ed. Stephen Spender (London, 1974), pp. 90–121.

of thinking but is frankly engaged in defining and distinguishing forms
of thought. The definition is conducted through moods of loving and
hating. The poem dares to name the feelings, love and dislike:

> Thought, I love thought.
> But not the jaggling and twisting of already existent ideas
> I despise that self-important game.
> Thought is the welling up of unknown life into consciousness,
> Thought is the testing of statements on the touchstone of the
>   conscience,
> Thought is gazing on to the face of life, and reading what can
>   be read,
> Thought is pondering over experience, and coming to conclusion.
> Thought is not a trick, or an exercise, or a set of dodges,
> Thought is a man in his wholeness wholly attending.

Definition and discussion is carried on through positive and negative
assertion, but not for long. One of the impressive features of the poem
is the way it leaves behind the statements of loving and disliking, and
the comparison of kinds of thought, for a series of impassioned definitions. Each is a grave meditation on thought, and the repetitions
increase the gravity. The urgent current of feeling is not that of argument or classification but praise. Each account of thought appreciates
the experience of thinking, and slowly the appreciation rises to the
height of the final sentence. The poem beautifully bears out everything
it asserts. Its thoughts and feelings well up into consciousness, it
ponders and slowly comes to its conclusion. Its language, while inclined
to be abstract, has enough physical suggestiveness to bear out the final
claim to wholeness. Hopkins thought that all poetry was love-poetry,
which is perhaps another way of claiming wholeness.

Narrative and dramatic forms in literature resemble the narrative
and dramatic forms of extra-literary behaviour. There is a less clear
but equally close connection between states of strong feeling and lyrical
forms of feeling, though what lyric perhaps cannot quite manage to
evoke is the inarticulate possession of feeling. In the life we live outside
poems feeling is not always articulate, but can also work through
touch, gesture and look. Lyric can get close to such silences, in the
spaces between phrases and phases of passion, and sometimes at the ends
of poems. It may be the very simplest lyric which aspires to such
rests and pauses, sometimes in a brooding refrain, and sometimes

through that brevity of which Yeats was a master, whose conclusion can breathe in silence:

> Wine comes in at the mouth
> And love comes in at the eye;
> That's all we shall know for truth
> Before we grow old and die.
> I lift the glass to my mouth,
> I look at you, and I sigh.

Perhaps most lyrics end in a reverberation of words, but some can move out of vibrant stillness into that familiar silence of strong feeling where words fail us.

2

Thinking and Feeling in the Songs and Sonnets of John Donne

Great lyric poetry like Donne's, makes us see what D. H. Lawrence meant when he complained that 'we have no language for the feelings'.[1] Lyric creates individual forms of emotional experience, freeing us from the fixities and definites of naming and classifying. Donne's shorter poems renew, recreate, and accessibly record the life of the passions, keeping faith with the way the passions grow, move, shift, combine, and relate to intelligence and sensation. Donne's very wide-ranging love-poems can be broken down into a catalogue of passions: they construct and elucidate desire, affection, fondness, closeness, tenderness, certainty, loving identification, yearnings, grief, exultation, celebration, longing, deprivation, loss, bitterness, scorn, contempt, loathing, hostility, frustration, jealousy, spite, revulsion, delight, excitement, bliss, rest. Such naming, however truthfully multiplied, is hopelessly inadequate, and I essay it in order to show its misleading crudity. It not only tells us very little, if anything, about the poetry, but goes right against the grain of poetry's passionate eloquence. Lyric creates a language for the passions by not naming, by showing those limits and falsities of naming which Lawrence derided:

> We see love, like a woolly lamb, or like a decorative decadent panther in Paris clothes: according as it is sacred or profane. We see hate, like a dog chained to a kennel. We see fear, like a shivering monkey. We see anger like a bull with a ring through his nose, and greed, like a pig. (op. cit. p. 756)

I want to look at three groups of poems in the light of this approach to lyric, my grouping being solely one of convenience. I shall look at one poem of satisfied and secure love, a few poems of hostility and

[1] 'The Novel and the Feelings', in *Phoenix*, ed. E. D. McDonald (London, 1936), p. 757.

frustration, and one poem which gives expression to a complex passion which affirms faith and entertains doubt. I want to suggest that all these poems, and others like them, insist on the complexity and fluidity of states of passion. Some of Donne's most secure assertions include or imply the negation of fulfilment, while some of his most hostile poems reveal the springs of cynicism in tenderness and caring. His poems are immensely concentrated, yet almost always speak from the total experience. They keep pace with the particularity of moment-to-moment existence, and also show the richness, and fullness, of the energetic imagination. His total eloquence speaks intelligently even in irrational or extreme states of passion, is playful when most profound, sensuous when most conceptual. This poetry is formally various too, possessing the advantage of lyric in being able to refuse or bypass the history and analysis of drama and narrative, and so productive of intensities and fluidity, yet using dramatic and narrative forms eclectically and realistically, as our consciousness outside art uses drama or story to shape its passionate recordings and desires. George Eliot said 'there is no human being who having both passions and thoughts does not think in consequence of his passions' (*Middlemarch*, ch. 47), and Donne not only illustrates this truth but shows an explicit awareness of it. For he is not only one of the most energetic lyric poets but also one of the most self-conscious. His poems are often shattering, like a blow without an excuse or an embrace without a problem, but they are also, as we know, vastly learned and self-aware. As Walton observed: 'His fancy was unimitably high, equalled only by his great wit; both being made useful by a commanding judgment'. The commanding judgment, however, is that of a poet.

Two quotations from Donne will be more economical than any reminders of T. S. Eliot on the united sensibility. In *The Progresse of the Soule* Donne speaks of 'the tender well-arm'd feeling braine' and in 'The Blossome' of 'A naked thinking heart'. These phrases perfectly express what we can call the 'interinanimation' (see 'The Exstasie') of passions and intellect. They draw attention, or may be used to draw attention, to the nakedness and vulnerability which we feel in some of these poems. History, psychology, and moral judgment are bypassed, we are strongly rooted in present time, the stress and rush of feeling is preserved, not lost to the 'commanding judgment': accordingly, we have a special sense of the exposure of human beings in their relationships. This is a feeling which also forms part of the response to

Shakespeare's sonnets, for instance, or to Lawrence's *Ship of Death* poems; and in these works is found the other quality which is central to Donne, the sense of pride, triumph, delight and power, felt by the artist but on behalf of a prowess and energy larger than the experience of art. Donne answers beautifully to Coleridge's description of Shakespearian wit as the overflow of artistic power, creativity exulting and scattering its energies, in a virtuosity which is never merely virtuosity.

'Loves Growth' shows Donne's wit, seriousness, sensuousness, profundity, and play. It is a restrained, though not narrow poem, remembered for its assertion that 'Love's not so pure, and abstract, as they use/To say, which have no Mistresse but their Muse', a couplet no reader or critic of Donne can afford to forget. If we try to describe the tones of feeling we find that the beginning of the first stanza is deceptively and teasingly cynical, dryly beginning, 'I scarce beleeve my love to be so pure' and not revealing its certainty and praise until the end of the sixth line. It reverses the pattern of many of the so-called cynical poems, which begin with deceptive praise or trust, to move disturbingly into rejection. The false start here belongs to a fine blend of levity and deep gravity which marks the whole poem. It is a poem which seems surprised by joy, and permitted by surprise and joy to play, delightedly and exhilaratingly:

> I scarce beleeve my love to be so pure
>   As I had thought it was,
>   Because it doth endure
> Vicissitude, and season, as the grasse;
> Me thinkes I lyed all winter, when I swore,
> My love was infinite, if spring make'it more.

This upward lift, from play to seriousness, is something that recurs through the poem, but one of the things that Donne teaches his reader is the danger of so fixing patterns of feeling. There are the recurring upward movements, but their differences are as important as their resemblances. The poem's second movement of rising is one which depends more on a contrast of images than on a suspension of argument. And the range of feeling covered is individual; the quick, almost painful glance at love's pain is remarkable for its stabbing brevity, and is present rather in the aside or parenthesis that insists on taking in the whole truth, than in any bold antithetical relation to the health, energy, and joy in the sun's 'working vigour'. The first stanza continues:

But if this medicine, love, which cures all sorrow
　　With more, not onely bee no quintessence,
　　But mixt of all stuffes, paining soule, or sense,
And of the Sunne his working vigour borrow,
Love's not so pure, and abstract, as they use
To say, which have no Mistresse but their Muse,
But as all else, being elemented too,
Love sometimes would contemplate, sometimes do.

The third upward lift, in these final four lines, is again new, being alto-
gether lighter, more amused than anything we have had up to now,
and concluding in the blunt simplicity of 'do' with that kind of rough
'masculine' force so characteristic of the third, eighteenth and nine-
teenth *Elegies*. The heart of the poem seems to lie in the beginning of
the second stanza, where the upward movement is most whole and
most joyous:

And yet not greater, but more eminent,
　　Love by the spring is growne;
　　As, in the firmament,
Starres by the Sunne are not inlarg'd, but showne.
Gentle love deeds, as blossomes on a bough,
From loves awaken'd root do bud out now.

The movement here is a gentle stir, like the particular sexual movement which is being invoked. It seems to emerge from the movement
from argument and scientific example, that of stars and sun, to the
natural and self-evident comparison with blossom; from the tiny lift
from simile (blossoms) to metaphor (root) which in turn blurs the
metaphorical into the literal; and from the emphasis on the gentle
stirring after the vigour, working, and 'doing' of the previous stanza.
In the concluding lines of the poem, there is a change from sensuousness to formality, generalisation and argument. Such a change is appropriate to the enlargement of time in the look at the future of winter
and other springs, and the enlargement of scale in the look at the public
world. We move into a new thought, that of a continuing increase
through the years, and a new claim, purchased after a harder look at
the seasonal conceit and a refusal to take the calendar's analogy too
literally. There is also the vigorous new spurt of wit in the ironic joke
about taxes; an unflattering argument, this, but immediately followed
by the serene and grave assurance of the last line:

And though each spring doe adde to love new heate,
As princes doe in times of action get
New taxes, and remit them not in peace,
No winter shall abate the springs encrease.

Each lifting motion is distinct, the whole poem consisting of a series of separated lifts, climbing like a smooth moving-stair. But we should be giving a very abstract account of the lyrical movement unless we said that there the praises, claims, and vows, are made in markedly differing moods, teasing, playful, witty, moving up to and away from the poem's heart, where the feeling is most sensuous, most gentle, most creative of beauty. The softness here seems to create a special intimacy, despite the total lack of personal address, and the intimate impression is ensured by the final movement into a larger area of wit and reference. The poem seems to achieve its unity by a final triumphant reach towards new and disparate material, ending on a flourish and a reassurance.

It is a staggering example of Donne's capacity for dropping and picking up wit and fancy, or, to put it another way, for using flights of wit and fancy audaciously, simply, and always passionately. His love-lyrics, like love, are eloquent both in extravagance and restraint. The quietest and most peaceful part of this poem depends on the surrounding vigour. It depends too on that literal invocation of the seasons with which the poem begins. The real world of nature is undescribed but taken for granted in the quiet references to 'season' and 'the grasse', which have not only the air of assuming what is present but also of assuming every man's common experience, every man's spring after his winter. But nature becomes more particularised in the sun's 'working vigour' and the imagery of stars, blossom, bough, and root. It is not very easy to say how the particularity is created, since there is no description, and all the natural items are barely mentioned, neither elaborated nor personified. Donne seems to interinanimate human nature and the larger vegetable and mineral world of the spring by blending his appreciation of both worlds. He rejoices in the sun's working vigour and the gentleness of the growth of flowers, blurring simile into metaphor by the spread of feeling for the beauty and tenderness of human sex and the beauty and tenderness of non-human fertility. The phallic feeling in 'loves awaken'd root' is astonishingly gentle, and belongs to a quiet feeling for the body's movement which is continued in the 'stir'd' of the water's ripples. The poem creates a rare impression by its very familiar seasonal image, succeeding in using the sun, flower, and water to enlarge, define and praise sexuality, but also in bestowing a sexual beauty on the non-human world. In the 'working vigour' and in 'loves awaken'd root' there is a phallic beauty which seems to appreciate the phenomenal world, and to convey an impression of unity and kinship. This sense of fusion is not only an imaginative achievement, in the most precise sense of the term, but a proof, palpable and splendid, of the poem's hopeful celebration of love's growth.

It is not a hopeful salute to wholeness made at the expense of dis-passionate wisdom. The winter life, the public world, the future seasons, are all there too, not only because, as Empson reminds us, things suggest their opposites but because Donne's frequent achievement is to remind us of opposition. He is always aware of the rest of experience, can combine passionate with dispassionate appraisal. Such acknowledg-ment of the other side of celebration is there in the sidelook at love's pain, which cures sorrow 'with more'. It is there too in the last airy flight of wit, which creates a movement away from the intimate phy-sical tenderness into the ordinary testing world, a flight earned and licensed by assurance and delight. On reflection, the final excursion seems also to continue the proof that love is 'mixt of all stuffes'. Donne's love-poetry, like love, is mixed of 'all stuffes', embracing aesthetic praise, sexual energy, urgency, gentleness, rest, ease, bluntness, gravity, play. Like so much great poetry, this is a poem aware of itself; its image of the water's spreading ripples applies to the poem's own outward reach and centre, its circles being also 'all concentrique'.

Donne's poetry of certain love has this inclusiveness. 'Sweetest love', 'The Good-morrow', 'Lecture upon the Shadow', 'The Computation' and 'The Relique', amongst other poems, all have this capacity for concentration and breadth. 'The Relique''s most gravely delighted tribute can include the 'cynical' parenthesis about womankind being 'to more then one a Bed'; the theme of that extraordinary poem, 'Negative Love', is in a way demonstrated in Donne's positive declara-tions, which show an awareness of the difficulty and danger of love in the larger world. At the same time, these positive love-poems par-ticularise intimacy with changing passion and sensuousness. The sen-suousness is various, to be sure, and at times resides less in local life of a detail than in a diffuse musicality, as in 'The Paradox', an almost abstract piece of witty argument where physicality is that of ordered sound, not that of invoked experience. Physicality, of one kind or another, is the rule in Donne. It belongs, however, not only to the positive love-poetry but also to what we may like to describe, albeit crudely and temporarily, as Donne's poetry of destructive and rejecting passion. 'Loves Diet' is a destructive poem, both in theme and passion, but has a purchase on wholeness. If 'Loves Growth' conveys the knowing, marginal sense of pain, winter, and dishonesty, 'Loves Diet' hurls its scorn so as to reveal scorn's loving origins. The way the poem moves (in both senses of that word) is through wit, ironic and derogatory, and repulsive sensations. Wit and sensation work together in the images of obesity—'combersome unwieldinesse', 'burdenous corpulence'—and the idea of sucking sweat instead of tears. Such images are presented as unattractive, visually and tactilely, and are also contemptuously argued: 'made it feed upon/That which love worst endures, *discretion*', or 'I let him see/'Twas neither very sound, nor meant to mee'. Sometimes the stroke of wit depends entirely on the strong sensations, as in the last stanza, where love can be called 'my buzard love', without argument, fitting in immediately with the imagery of flight, recall, and sport, but taking its contempt and its offensiveness in its culminating definition of the food of love as carrion. The poem is a most serious act of rejection, and also in a sense about itself. It works through great control and economy, forcing resentment out in these physical and cerebral ways, until the release of the last stanza. At the end the imagery of the diet is dropped once the 'buzard' makes its logic felt. The feeling is one of release, the poem now exhibiting the ease and heartless play it has been attempting in the diet:

> Thus I reclaim'd my buzard love, to flye
> At what, and when, and how, and where I chuse;
>   Now negligent of sport I lye,
>   And now as other Fawkners use,
> I spring a mistresse, sweare, write, sigh and weepe:
> And the game kill'd, or lost, goe talke, and sleepe.

The state of not caring, of cutting love down to size, of 'lowering' it, has only been achieved slowly, through the whole poem, and the marked disappearance of contempt and irony in the sense of freedom makes it very clear that the '*odi*' is part of the '*amo*'. In contrast and change it has created for us the sense that value has existed, and must be destroyed. The hostile feeling, and the devaluation of love shows the process of cynical feeling, and creates an apology for it. Better a buzzard than this kind of falcon?

Donne's so-called cynical poems seem to reveal cynicism, to show it as something created. I am not trying to argue it out of existence in order to claim a life-affirming creativity, but rather to suggest that destructiveness is shown as the other side of love, in the poetic process.

Donne gives an anatomy of his passions, analytic and dissecting. He does much more than convey the knowledge that jealousy and cynicism are love soured, frustrated, or cheated. He creates the process of the passion, writing about starving his love, and dramatising the effort and the success in active verse. Another example is 'The Blossome', much less sensuous than 'Loves Diet' but also a very dynamic poem. It begins very playfully and coolly, describing the blossom which has no knowledge of its brief mortality. Then it slowly moves into a statement of passion in the second stanza, which describes the heart through the parallel with the flower, the more coolly and slowly for separating the means from the end. It is a much more quietly reasoning poem of rejection than 'Loves Diet'. Its argument is made at first more in pity than in anger, using the sad self-conscious reflection, 'But thou which lov'st to bee/Subtile to plague thy selfe'. Love was a passive, non-answering character in 'Loves Diet' and the drama was one of action, not debate. This is a poem of dramatic argument, working through question and answer, though with a strongly embodied physicality. One of its achievements is that of making the concept physical, in 'A naked thinking heart'. It also makes the physical scornfully present by the understatement, 'Practise may make her know some other part'. And there is one line of direct sensuality, 'thou shalt see/Mee fresher, and more fat, by being with men,/Then if I had staid still with her and thee'. Once more the last verse casts off the effort, though here in a forecast, not a recorded achievement. We seem to be still mastered by the emotion that tries to reason itself out of existence:

> For Gods sake, if you can, be you so too:
>   I would give you
>   There, to another friend, whom wee shall finde
>   As glad to have my body, as my minde.

Donne's drama allows him to acknowledge the complex sensibility. He calls the heart 'subtile' and 'thinking', avoids a dialogue between mind and heart, discusses parts and organs, but plainly speaks from and to human complexity. The dramatic form is made particularised and generalised through wit. Wit says that the 'naked thinking heart, that makes no show' can have no meaning for a woman who has no experience of such purity. But wit is also strikingly absent in the simple direct thrust of 'naked thinking heart'. The wit may be subtle, as in the comment about subtlety, or crude, as in the aggressive joke about 'some other part' or in the quieter stroke,

> You goe to friends, whose love and meanes present
>   Various content
> To your eyes, eares, and tongue, and every part.

The word 'double entendre' tells us nothing about Donne's sexual references out of context, since each one works locally and particularly, as an 'organ to the whole'.

'The Blossome' ends with a clearing away of wit in plain statement, and seems at least about to achieve a victory. The all-important conclusion to Donne's poems has been emphasised by Helen Gardner in the quotation from Donne's sermon, 'the force of the whole piece is for the most part left to the shutting . . . the last clause is as the impression of the stamp'. We often find this kind of reduction of wit, sometimes as here with the conclusion of a particular debate or argument, just before the poem ends, sometimes as, in 'A Valediction: of my Name in the Window', with an extremely self-conscious reflection about wit, like the epilogue to a play. At times the end is co-terminous with the very last word, as in another poem of hostile love, 'The Legacie'. This is also a poem where a bizarre physicality of description plays in with the wit. The 'naked thinking heart' combines two meanings: that of 'naked and yet thinking' with 'nakedly thinking'. 'The Legacie' also plays elaborately with the conceit of the heart, with a detailed psychology and physiology. The wit, drama, and sensuousness all belong to Donne, but all also singularly and uniquely belong to this poem. The speaker here assumes something of that clarity, purity, and innocence which belonged to the heart in 'The Blossome', and achieves a double impact: it impersonates a purely believing love and makes way for the knowing disillusionment. In 'The Legacie' the speaker never loses the innocence, though the poem's last line has that kind of Swiftian irony which makes it possible for us to take the speaker either as innocently not reflecting on the irony, or as sophisticatedly assuming it.

The poem begins quietly, explanatorily, deceptively, sounding simply the tones of what might be happy love, a sadness belonging to any separation:

> When I dyed last, and Deare, I dye
>   As often as from thee I goe,
>   Though it be an houre agoe,
> And Lovers houres be full eternity . . .

There follows, still without showing its hand (or heart) the first conceit about the imagined (or dreamed) death, legacy, executor, and will. Only when the poem is complete do we know the full significance of the death and of the brilliantly blurred self-excusing and other-accusing, 'Tell her anon,/That my selfe, that's you, not I,/Did kill me'; of the legacy of the heart; of the goodwill and astonishment of the executor who tried to locate the legacy and 'could there finde none'. The striking feature of the movement here is its extreme slowness, as the speaker demonstrates the difference between real hearts and false ones, false ones being really so unlike the real thing that they cannot be mistaken for it by the anatomist:

> But I alas could there finde none,
>   When I had ripp'd me,'and search'd where hearts should lye;
> It kill'd mee'againe that I who still was true,
> In life, in my last Will should cozen you.
>
> Yet I found something like a heart,
>   But colours it, and corners had,
>   It was not good, it was not bad,
> It was intire to none, and few had part.
> As good as could be made by art
>   It seem'd, and therefore for our losses sad,
> I thought to send that heart in stead of mine,
> But oh, no man could hold it, for twas thine.

The physical violence in the action of ripping and searching, and the emotional violence in the description of artifice, are the more forceful for being presented in the tones of quiet innocence, goodwill, pain, and patient examination. The quiet thoughtfulness not only draws out the tension but also makes its own innocence eloquently felt, in the bewildered, step-by-step discovery: first there is no heart where there should have been one, in the usual place, then, after all, 'something like' a heart. The description, 'colours it, and corners', belongs to the scrutiny of the patient examining eye, while loudly sounding the duplicities. The distance travelled is so great that the final explanation comes with tremendous force. Added to the force is that also of the completed argument: the heart was artificial, it was impossible for any man to hold it, 'for twas thine'. The double argument re-doubles climax, one point taken in a moment after another. The heart's physical substance is so strongly established that it seems to have become a monstrous incarnation, with allegorical and visceral strengths, both relevant to the rational analysis and to the final contemptuous insult. But once more, hostility is revealed as the end of a slow-dying love. The poem is not simply hostile.

If poems impersonating such different moods and passions all imply this wisdom about the other side of experience, it is not surprising that some of the *Songs and Sonnets* resist this classification into positive and negative. But I want to suggest that those poems which do resist are very rare imaginative achievements; it being rather more common, both in life and in the concentrated form of lyric, to create and act out specialised passions. Passionate experience, however it may possess and transcend knowledge and irony, tends towards singleness. But Donne wrote a few poems which possess a rare and highly disturbing quality, which belong to and imprint that kind of passionate experience which joins extremes, which feels the momentary truth of possession with the possibility of loss, the expectation of denial at the time of recognition. A poem of this kind is 'A Valediction: of my Name in the Window'. Like 'Loves Growth' it is both very intense and very self-reflective, consciously remarking its own flights of wit and fantasy. Donne's very many literary-critical generalisations within his poetry, about wit, feeling, form, fantasy, dream, plain and ornate forms, and art, are of considerable interest, and they are accompanied, like similar large generalisations in Shakespeare, Milton, Keats, Wordsworth, or T. S. Eliot, by illuminating local self-references. Just as Donne observes the connection between subtlety and torment, in 'The Blossome', so in this 'Valediction' he draws our attention to a connection between fantasy and distress. Neither connection belongs exclusively to art or nature, which explains why at times we may not know whether to call some of this passionate poetry very artful or very natural.

'A Valediction: of my Name in the Window' begins by creating a pattern of wit and qualification. The first four lines of the first stanza argue that the signature scratched in the lady's window can stand as a sign of his constancy, but its last two lines shift the argument to assert that what will really give the signature value is not his quality, but her eye. The second begins by arguing that the glass of the window can stand for his transparent candour: 'As all confessing, and through-shine as I', but goes on to say that it can also reflect her image, and, finally that more important than these separate reflections is the signature's emblem of their unity, 'Here you see mee, and I am you'. This setting up and putting down of argument and emblem does not continue, in such neat stanzaic form, but once established as a pattern goes on more irregularly, spreading qualification over the whole of the third stanza and becoming very self-reflective in the fourth,

> Of if too hard and deepe
> This learning be, for a scratch'd name to teach,
> It, as a given deaths head keepe,
> Lovers mortalitie to preach,
> Or thinke this ragged bony name to bee
> My ruinous Anatomie.

The self-consciousness about 'This learning', arguing for a change of emblem, draws attention to the poem's shape-changing, which in itself, as often in Donne, gives the effect of restlessness and a loose-sitting exercise of choice, 'Take this or this or this'. But the looseness and eclecticism is compatible with deep seriousness, as in the analogy with the resurrection of the body, in stanzas five, six and seven. In the eighth stanza we move from the pattern of proffered and shifting emblems to a sustained fantasy, in which the signature is cast for certain passive and active roles. The habit of wit having been established in the comparisons, the fantasy is perhaps also presented as something possible, something entertained, a subject for the mind to play with. The fantasy also involves a change from the early images of steadfastness to the image of infidelity, all the early emblems depending indeed on her 'eye', her use of the signature as memorial and promise, the imagined infidelity depending on her neglect of these significances.

The infidelity, or its approach, is imaged in considerable dramatic psychological, and physical detail:

> When thy'inconsiderate hand
> Flings out this casement, with my trembling name,

> To looke on one, whose wit or land,
> 　New battry to thy heart may frame,
> 　Then thinke this name alive, and that thou thus
> 　　In it offendst my Genius.

The wit is that of very compressed and various point: the signature's 'trembling' is justified because the scratched characters are irregular, not smooth; because the window itself shakes with the gesture of its opening; because it represents his image, trembling with insecurity, doubt, and fear; because of the shock of the act even of imagined treachery; and because of the imagined new love's energy, 'New battry'. All combine to give physicality to the central idea of a shattered love. There follows the small inset drama, very fully imagined, of the seduction: the maid, the persuasion, the gold, the page, the letter at the pillow, all eloquent and the more eloquent for the central speaking omission of the new lover. Suspension and ellipsis are present also in the penultimate stanza where we are led to expect a sexual climax, but are instead held, with tension and decorum, at the point where she is writing an answer to her new lover's letter

> 　　And if this treason goe
> 　To'an overt act . . .

It begins, only to be let down, in this poem about writing, in the discovery that the 'act' is writing, sufficiently bad as a betrayal of the significant act of writing, which by now has for lady and for reader been charged with all the argued values and meanings. We also stop short, anguished, of the unimaginable act. In actual argument, there comes the check as the speaker thinks that perhaps the name's magic will work, not just as fancy or conceit but indeed as a good psychological cause, a pre-Freudian error of guilt and love which will write the wrong name—a marvellous touch, combining fancy and reality in a way utterly typical of Donne:

> 　So, in forgetting thou remembrest right,
> 　　And unaware to mee shalt write.

It is then as if he stops short in the flight of fancy, realising after all that a mere name is a feeble device and guard against infidelity. So the last stanza undermines the fantasy, as the earlier local wit-points were undermined. Fantasy is questioned, then wit, and ultimately, the whole poetic act:

> But glasse, and lines must bee,
> No meanes our firme substantiall love to keepe;
> Neere death inflicts this lethargie,
> And this I murmure in my sleepe;
> Impute this idle talke, to that I goe,
> For dying men talke often so.

The argument is blatantly disingenuous, still using that same wit and fancy it rejects, arguing the firmness and substantiality of their love from the fragility of the glass, denying and yet incorrigibly keeping up the play of fancy and wit. The rejection of the poem, however, makes the strongest claim after all, as the speaker says that he is talking madly but decorously, not in command but driven to irrationality by the anguish of parting. The argument is of course made most wittily, parting seen as 'death' and the lover dying. The final effect, recasting and revising the total experience of the poem, and taking force and point from the initial habit of self-questioning wit, is to establish a sense of reality by rejecting art. It confers a kind of reality on glass, signature, room, lovers, and parting, in one of those admissions of illusion, like Cressida's speech about her truth, or Hamlet's ghost in the cellarage, or Keats's 'warm scribe, my hand', that oddly but powerfully distinguish art and the live act of creating art. Here in a new last bizarre liveliness is the admission of the poem as artefact and as reality, for 'lines' apply both to signature and verses, while 'murmure', 'idle talke' and 'talke often so' all apply more to the poem than to the local conceit, though taking us out of poetry into talk.

The motion is circular. The poem cannot efface its tracks: poet, lover, woman, reader, have been through the fantasy, and if what the imagination seizes as beauty must be truth, so what it seizes as horror must also be truth. The inclusiveness and duality of this poem is violent and pathetic, stating both the extreme conviction that love is firm and reliable, needing no emblems or promises, and the opposite vision of doubt, fear, and jealousy. It moves between and joins the need to persuade with the fantasy that explains the act of persuasion. Poet, like lover and lunatic, and here most precisely impersonating all three identities, has both reality and fantasy, and can have both without commitment to either. Or, to put it in a way that makes sense not only of our feeling that this art reveals the torments as well as the riches of imagination, he has to have reality and fantasy, is forced by passion to imagine all the possibilities, and in hateful detail. Urgency, strain, grief, affection, security, insecurity, jealousy, faith, strength, and weakness all acted out, in a unity that belongs both to art and to experience. Donne is explicit about such wholeness in another poem, 'A Valediction: of the Booke':

> To take a latitude
> Sun, or starres, are fitliest view'd
> At their brightest, but to conclude
> Of longitudes, what other way have wee,
> But to marke when, and where the darke eclipses bee?

I am very far from wishing to smuggle in an argument about the biographical origins[1] of Donne's poetry. What this range and variety of passionate lyric tells us, if we need to be told, is that the imagination, passion and intelligence which belong to poetry, and which are both displayed and discussed in Donne, do not belong only to poetry.

---

[1] Not because I doubt them, but because lengthy argument on the subject would be out of place here.

3

Clough's Self-Consciousness

To speak of Clough's modernity is understandable but misleading. Perhaps no other Victorian writer is so visibly imprisoned in his Victorianism, breathing with difficulty under its glass dome. The breathing, the difficulty, the restraints and the visibility, are all found in his poetry. His idealism, his doubts about his idealism, his troubled sexuality, his ethical brooding, his views of work and political action, all would of course have taken different forms had he truly been a modern, but the play of his passion and his intelligence brings him close to us.

Richard Gollin's remarks on Clough always command respect, and in a review of two recent books in *Victorian Studies* (x. 3, March 1967) he takes Paul Veyriras to task for 'occasionally mistaking Clough's moral concern for his personal compulsion'. I have to begin by admitting that I find myself unable to feel as confident as Mr Gollin about distinguishing Clough's detached and controlled criticism from his 'self-directed utterances'. While acknowledging Clough's variousness and toughness, I see his analytic mode as inextricably bound up with his personal compulsions, and indeed welcome his attachment to the personal as a source of warmth and acceptance even in satire. In this essay I want to emphasise in turn three aspects of the poetry: its lyric structure; its use of narrative; and its intellectual argument and analysis. Since I see Clough's strength in his combination of lyric with argument, narrative with lyric, and irony with passion, there will be some overlap and repetition.

I

Clough's lyrical utterance is given its intensity by being connected with a full sense of life in a way that usually works against the lyric grain. Lyric poetry, like George Eliot's Lydgate, often raves on the heights, cut off from the habitual self that waits below. Clough's strength of feeling is not bought at the expense of his habitual self.

His characteristic breadth and awareness is plain in the well-known letter to Blanche Smith, which he wrote in 1852, two years before they married:

> Fortified by bread and cheese I return and rise to the sublime . . .
> here in this dim deceitful misty moon-shiny night-time of existence
> we grope about and run up against each other, and peer blindly but
> enquiringly into strange faces, and sooner or later (for comfort's sake
> for the night is cold you see and dreary) clasp hands and make vows
> and choose to keep together and withdraw again sometimes and
> wrench away hands and seize others and do we know not what. . .
> (quoted by Katharine Chorley, *Arthur Hugh Clough: The Un-
> committed Mind*, Oxford, 1962, p. 235)

It is true: he does rise to the sublime, here and in his poetry, and his sublime is a matter of concept and feeling, and seems to achieve the heroic by refusing the heights. The qualities of the human being are the qualities of the poet. There is his candour, warmer than most candour; his toughness, gentler than most toughness; and his affection-ateness, more scrupulous than most affectionateness. There is the ability to analyse and still appreciate, criticise and still celebrate. He dissects feeling while feeling, and the pains of exposure and probe become part of what is felt. His materials are transformed by the act of inspection, as in all genuine science and genuine poetry.

The vivisective impulse is what Joyce saw as essentially part of the modern spirit. In Clough it is never a matter of the mind operating on the heart. One of Gerard Manley Hopkins's best sonnets, 'My own heart let me more have pity on', is an excellent model for critics of Clough as well as for critics of Hopkins:

> My own heart let me more have pity on; let
> Me live to my sad self hereafter kind,
> Charitable; not live this tormented mind
> With this tormented mind tormenting yet.

In this poem the poet struggles visibly against the temptation to diagnose conflict in the facile terms of a heart/mind antithesis. He begins by dividing 'my own heart' from 'me', then speaks of the object of the pity as 'my sad self', and then sets against this expansion the notion of the 'tormented mind' tormenting not a heart, nor a self, but 'this tormented mind' itself. Clough is like Hopkins in his refusal to condense the difficulties of being human into a conflict between intellect and feeling. He sets out the difficulty of analysis and diagnosis, and the difficulty becomes part of the pain and effort. His is a typically modern inability to identify the problem, and it is an inability which often creates poetic forms which shuttle to and fro, or which are tortured in convolution rather than progressive and developmental. The only one of his three fine long poems to have a progressive form is *The Bothie of Tober-Na-Vuolich*, and its progression towards an affirmative conclusion depends on an outline, a fable, rather than on a full exploration of an action or a complex picture of living. *The Bothie* has its beginning, middle, and end, but its form is a foreshortened, erratic, and collapsed form. The other two long poems, *Amours de Voyage*, and *Dipsychus*, are convoluted and even circular in form, and their conclusions, if that is the right word, do not seem to complete a development. Clough's forms of poetry come out of the honest experiments of his strong passions and intelligence; they present more than usual feeling in frank disorder. He writes from the centre of his doubts and anguish and this often means that the poems seem to lack a centre. It is no wonder that we compulsively call him modern.

Disorder in Clough comes both from an inability to work through to a final answer, and from a related inability to isolate the experiences of belief, desire, ideal, and dream. What struck some of his friends— Matthew Arnold, for instance, when he had begun to 'settle down' and of course Mrs Clough—as an excessive fastidiousness and fussiness in analysis and scruple, may strike us as fine refusal to compromise, to lie, or to live partially. Clough's tenderness of conscience is visible in his arguments about idealism and in his approach to the practical commerce of living. My formulation immediately hardens into falsity under the glare of Clough's *lumen siccum*: he so seldom felt able to say what was ideal and what was practical. The apparent 'ideal' might be fantasy luring us away from work and action, while 'practical demands' might borrow the peremptory voice of duty in order to disguise the solicitations of passion and worldliness. In a pre-Freudian world, Clough is painfully alert to the masks which desires can wear, and most of his poetry is an analytic attempt to strip down the masks, for he knows that human beings can wear them in layers, may be made up of them. The analysis is not performed by the clear exercise of reasoning and logic: he admits the pain, fatigue, hope, hopelessness, frustration,

longing, doubt, and fear of the analytic process. The feelings are seen
and discovered as analysts and as analysands.

The double self, as he calls it in *Dipsychus* (whose title and form at
once conflict[1] to show up the crudeness of concepts of mere duality)
is most simply present in the love-letter I have quoted. He sets down
the bread and cheese then rises to the sublime. Having set down in
duality and tension what he is doing, he then does it. He composes an
image which is *also* divided: in 'the dim deceitful misty moonshiny
night-time' there is the cold, the obscurity, the need and isolation, but
there is also allure and beauty. Moreover, moonshine has perhaps helped
to make the image, which looks cynical at first glance but turns out to
have a Platonic tinge of hopefulness in its implied possibility of daylight.
The shiftiness of this image, and the self-consciousness of its setting-
down are found everywhere in Clough's poetry. He warned Blanche
that her heart was not 'a priceless treasure' and told her not to dream of
'everlasting unions and ties that no change can modify'. Change and
modification are conspicuous in his poems. His analysis proceeds by
setting up a pattern and then qualifying it.

Sometimes the sense of modification is compressed into a single
complex image like the ambivalent moonshine, as in the cutting second
line of this almost (but only almost) innocuous hymnlike list of human
qualities:

> A mind for thoughts to pass into,
> A heart for loves to travel through,
> Five senses to detect things near,
> Is this the whole that we are here?
>
> ('What we, when face to face')

Sometimes it is set up in a polarity, as in the 'double' dreams of Cain
in 'The Song of Lamech', where we move from one extreme to
another, or in the movement from a narrow winding street to the top
of the campanile, in *Dipsychus*, or in Claude's labyrinth, in *Amours de
Voyage*, where he feels lost but keeps the 'clue' in his 'bosom unbroken',
or in the sinking fall through a fissure where he still feels 'the strength
of invisible arms up above me'. It would be easy to pile up instances.
But it is not only in imagery that we find the duality, tension and
contradiction. It is there in his elaborate structures of feeling, in the

---

[1] I take the poem to be an argument and struggle *between* the divided *Dipsychus*
and the ambiguous Spirit.

ordering and patterns of his 'sense of musical delight', in the refrains
which can give a specious sense of stability and a profound sense of
mutability, in his habit of quotation and self-quotation, in his fluency
and variations, his metrical power and self-consciousness about pro-
sody: 'Hexameters, by all that's odious', as the Spirit says. Clough uses
lyric analytically.

He can pose form against form, in a truly lyric argument, not only
when he makes Shakespeare answer Dipsychus's revolted

> But to be swilled with animal delight
> And yield five minutes' pleasure to the male—

with

> It was a lover and his lass

but when he puts the gravity of the rhyming hexameter

> Yes, it is beautiful ever, let foolish men rail at it never.
> Yes, it is beautiful truly, my brothers, I grant it you duly.

against the Spirit's

> How light we move, how softly! Ah,
> Tra lal la la, the gondola!

One of the most moving and powerful examples of integral lyric
argument is from *Ambarvalia*:

> Why should I say I see the things I see not,
>   Why be and be not?
> Show love for that I love not, and fear for what I fear not?
> And dance about to music that I hear not?
>   Who standeth still i' the street
>   Shall be hustled and justled about;
> And he that stops i' the dance shall be spurned by the dancers'
>   feet,—
> Shall be shoved and be twisted by all he shall meet,
>   And shall raise up an outcry and rout;
>   And the partner, too,—
>   What's the partner to do?

Clough argues in image and motion: the sick distaste for pretence and
conformity shows itself in the monotonous and insistent rhymes and

repetitions of the first four lines, and then arrests the flow abruptly and discordantly; but the argument moves, we leave the deflating image of the compulsive crowd and its threats and obstacles for the possibility of harmony. Clough moves through the marvellous fragmentary 'And the partner, too,—/What's the partner to do?' into an image of real hearing and responsive movement in 'the living dance'. He reaches the odd conclusion that the thing to do is to keep moving in imitative fashion 'amid the throng', waiting for the music to become audible—except that Clough's perception always races ahead of his readers, and just as we catch up with the point about the temporary conformity, turning and bounding not to nothing but to a music to be made by the expectant soul, his suggestion is eroded by doubt, and replaced by the melancholy beating question,

> Alas! alas! alas! and what if all along
> The music is not sounding?

In the second part of the poem Clough revises image and music, and poses the existence of two musics, one loud and coarse, the other 'soft and low,/Stealing whence we do not know'. Clough constantly trips our expectation, whether it is the expectation of heart or the reason, and the distinction here is characteristically cross-hatched. The first music is not the public music of conformity and social harmony, it is bred from fancy and only sounds in the head; the second music is 'easily forgot', and we must keep the ear alert, painfully, and not listen to any other sound,

> But listen, listen, listen,—if haply be heard it may;
> Listen, listen, listen,—is it not sounding now?

In the last stanza the image of sight joins that of sound, to present something like Arnold's 'bolt shot back' on the buried self,

> Yea, and as thought of some beloved friend
> By death or distance parted will descend,
> Severing, in crowded rooms ablaze with light,
> As by a magic screen, the seër from the sight
> (Palsying the nerves that intervene
> The eye and central sense between);
> So may the ear,
> Hearing, not hear,

Though drums do roll, and pipes and cymbals ring;
So the bare conscience of the better thing
Unfelt, unseen, unimaged, all unknown,
May fix the entrancèd soul 'mid multitudes alone.

The poem dissolves and rejects its own imagery, and Clough's word 'conscience', into which is gathered the senses of moral and aesthetic consciousness, has to stand 'bare', its object 'unfelt, unseen' like Keats's unheard music. The poem works by its own momentum, like all good poetry, and its address to the ear and eye, like its tone and pattern, moves a considerable distance in these three stanzas. Clough's ability to shift feeling over such distances within an individual form which is sufficiently an enclosure to define and imprint, makes his lyrics remarkable and disconcerting. This poem sets up a music, sharp and intricate, and transforms it into something slower, heavier, more confused and groping, while using the same set of instruments—question and answer, the pivoting 'yets', the anticipations and echoes. Eventually, with no flourishes or triumphant climax, we move out of the high-pitched lamentations and exhausted sighs, and the solicitous and affectionate advisings and hopes, into a recognition and an answer. It is not a metaphysical answer, either to questions of faith in the human or the more than human, because Clough's imagery has allowed him to be expansive and vague, to accommodate all or any of these questions in the structure and symbolism of music and the 'entrancèd soul'. The formal continuity and argument is made out of the ordering of feelings.

Not only do image and music set up such complex movement within individual poems, but can be seen across the poems, in larger correspondences and conversations. Clough quotes 'Easter Day' and *Amours de Voyage* in *Dipsychus*, and often revises, continues, and answers earlier poems. This cohesiveness is perhaps more unusual than we might expect, considering the nature of his poetry, and it seems to be a direct result of writing right from the human centre: all Clough's poems are equally grave and personal and—I believe—always deal with the same problems. There is no sense of dramatic striving for variety, or of conspicuous creation of separate beautiful pieces. Each poem performs an analysis of the passions and the intelligence by the passions and the intelligence and the process goes on and on. The poems send out sensitive antennae to each other, and come to create a body of work which has the integrity and wholeness of a man's diary or his correspondence: every piece is a whole and urgent message straight from the centre of suffering heart and mind. In the winding melancholy and sternness of 'Easter Day, Naples, 1849'[1] and the briefer, more static and emotionally unvaried reply, by 'another voice' in 'Easter Day II', in the echo of 'Jacob's Wives' at the very end of *The Bothie*, and in 'Bethesda's' answer to the first poem in *Ambarvalia*, the relations are those of resonant echo and qualification, not of contrast and argument. These poems move us through a sense of continuity and of increasing complication. Clough's assertions are so unassertive, so eroded by nuance and scruple, that there is not much scope for strong antithesis. In the first poem in *Ambarvalia*, for instance, one of the spirits insists that he will do his duty, though when asked if this means that he will participate or stand back from life, he says that he does not know. In 'Bethesda', in which the same spirits lie in sick hope round the pool that might be Lethe or Philosophy, the same spirit now does know, and knows that he will serve 'the world's desires', but has forgotten the word 'duty', now feels that he must do as other men do. The sequel puts the emphasis on fatigue—the spirit and the poet have lived that much longer—and on not knowing. But the first poem was not all that certain, and indeed also said, in one voice, 'I know not' and in another, 'I also know not, and I need not know'. In the sequel the 'I know not' is quoted and repeated, and reinforced in its sad weakness by the poet's 'I saw not, neither know', on which the poem fades out. The conversations between poems do not mark progress: 'Easter Day II' is 'another voice' and its assertion is posed flatly against the wretchedness of the long and elaborate structure of feeling of the first poem, at the end of which we have moved only reluctantly into a sense of 'reality', like prisoners changing prisons. The second poem presents another view, shows the imagination's activity in entertaining different stances.

[1] Mr Gollin, in the review already mentioned (*Victorian Studies*, x. 3 March 1967), disagrees with Veyriras's reading of the poem as an expression of poignant suffering and tells us that it is 'a consoling statement about anachronistic suffering'. I read the poems as a movement from poignant suffering towards consolation, and this movement is what I would call typically Cloughian: the sense of doubt's suffering is eroded but not removed by the consolations of rationality, and the poem's complex feeling is dynamically melancholy, sympathetic and tough.

II

Although Clough is a fine lyric poet, his central form is of course narrative, and his long poems are built up out of the non-progressive conversation we find in the shorter lyrics. Like the lyrics they accrete contrarieties and qualifications, and do not move towards climax and conclusion. But they are, of course, essentially *narrative* poems in which Clough tries out the different stances, relativities and possibilities in invented action and character, and in impersonated dialogue. *The Bothie,* *Amours de Voyage,* and *Dipsychus* are lyrical narratives, and have the toughness of hybrids. It is important to recognise the lyrical element because Clough is often regarded as a novelist in verse, just as he is often taken as an intellectual, rather than an emotional poet. He is very unlike a novelist, and especially unlike a Victorian novelist. His motion is very erratic, his fluidity and foreshortening and shuttling are all products of an essentially lyrical and musical form, where history is cut down so that feeling is prominent. He is less of a novelist than the other Victorian poets: to go from *The Ring and the Book,* for all its relativism, to *Dipsychus,* is like going from *Stephen Hero* to *The Portrait of the Artist as a Young Man,* from a full view of developed characters and actions to an intense and deliberately obscured selection. Both Browning and Tennyson tell much more complete and coherent stories and have a far greater range of psychological and emotional impersonation, though of course neither is a novelist in verse, and their narrative poems are both more and less than stories versified. 'Tithonus' and 'Œnone' also cut down narrative to emphasise moments of feeling, though these are of course poems where Tennyson can rely on the familiarity of mythological sources. Browning invents more freely, but his favourite monologue form both announces and keeps to its consistent selection. Clough's story-telling is much more disordered and foreshortened than Browning's or Tennyson's. His selections of character are wayward and at first sight arbitrary. He does not tell whole stories (except in *Mari Magno,* by far the least interesting of his big poems) and if we said that he created four characters, we should be exaggerating.

The poems are narratives but they are also lyrical. The lyrical element predominates, though both narrative and lyric express and form his drive towards passionate scrutiny and modification. *The Bothie, Amours de Voyage,* and *Dipsychus,* all contain within themselves the reason why they are so and not otherwise, why they are neither pure lyrics nor

developed narratives. I have mentioned the distinction Joyce makes in
A Portrait of the Artist as a Young Man between the three literary stages,
lyric, epical, and dramatic. Joyce's second stage, the epical, is distinguished from the simple lyric outcry and the impersonalised dramatic
form, and fits Clough quite well:

> The lyrical form is in fact the simplest verbal gesture of an instant
> of emotion, a rhythmical cry such as ages ago cheered on the man
> who pulled at the oar or dragged stones up a slope. He who utters
> it is more conscious of the instant of emotion than of himself as
> feeling emotion. The simplest epical form is seen emerging out of
> lyrical literature when the artist prolongs and broods upon himself
> as the centre of an epical event and this form progresses till the
> centre of emotional gravity is equidistant from the artist himself and
> from others. The narrative is no longer purely personal. The person-
> ality of the artist passes into the narration itself, flowing round and
> round the persons and the action like a vital sea. (pt. 5)

In order to see the lyric pressure, we have to say what Clough does
with narrative. In *The Bothie*, which is that rare thing, a virile and
inartificial pastoral, he outlines a fable about sexual desire and radical
discontent. The hero moves through two unsuitable and opposite loves
to find his last and right love. Where a novel would thrive on the social
and psychological developments, and show each environment and character in some detail, Clough's poem has lyrical not narrative propor-
tions and emphasis. He shows just a little, and indirectly, of Katie,
Philip's first love, though he does show the sensual passion, remorse and
rejection; he shows nothing at all of Lady Maria, his second love, and
describes rather than discusses his feeling for her in a curiously polemic
outburst which utters the extreme of feeling for a socially privileged
beauty in language and passion that admit their own proximity to
irony:

> While thou art eating black bread in the poisonous air of thy
>   cavern,
> Far away glitters the gem on the peerless neck of a Princess,
> Dig, and starve, and be thankful; it is so, and thou hast been
>   aiding.
>   Often I find myself saying, in irony is it, or earnest?
> Yea, what is more, be rich, O ye rich! be sublime in great houses. . .

He can teeter between commitment and irony, because the episode is all done in report, so that we are most conveniently cut off from the lady and the relationship, and, indeed, from any analysis of feeling. All we have is the outburst which does not quite know how to take itself, but does well enough to suggest a social and sexual contrast, necessary to the happy rapid fable and to the treatment of feeling. The poem concentrates on Elspie, and her character and person, socially just right, lovely, intelligent, even bookish (being Scots), are the more plausible for existing in a poem, not in a novel. The three characters and actions of the love-story are usefully foreshortened for the negative advantage of the fable, but also for the positive advantages of expressing sensation and feeling. The natural landscape is much more prominent than character and social contrast and it is there to bring out the needs and strengths and beauty of young desire, 'the natural man revealing'. Trees, glens, granite jambs, water, brightness and a sense of strong movement and able action are all profoundly expressive parts of the poem. The hexameters can rush and throb, while the landscape gives a necessary strength and grace, while the walking and swimming give nakedness, energy, beauty and masculinity. It is these sensations and feelings, not the actions and psychological details, that make the impact and point of the poem. As a fable it is as unlikely and facile and optimistic as some of the tales told in *Mari Magno*, but as a spirited lyric which sympathetically creates the movement, tension and climaxes of sensuality, it is entirely successful.

Amours de Voyage and *Dipsychus* are frankly introverted forms for analysis. In their stories we see character and action rather dimly. In *Amours de Voyage*, character is filtered through an epistolary form in which once again we find foreshortening and distancing. There is some sense of character, but very little detail of personality and relationship. Action is fittingly filtered through the introspective reverie in which Claude thinks out and round and through his passion until action is postponed, inhibited, and impeded. *Amours de Voyage* could not be simply a monologue: it needs enough shift in point of view to establish certain things outside the unreliable sensitive register of Claude's consciousness. It is important to see Mary Trevellyn's changing view of him. This establishes him as having a certain warmth and strength, in what she says about him as a person, and as a solid identity, because she says it, in her independently dramatised point of view. It establishes her too, outside the emotional analysis of Claude's letters: the direct play of her spirit, intelligence, tenderness, and tolerance make the poem larger, more concrete, and sadder than it could have been in an enclosed monologue. There is a sense of the largeness of the world, outside Claude's introspection, of the solid reality of love and this woman. The sense of loss is accordingly greater, though the lyrical concentration on Claude himself, at the beginning, gives the right kind of density and claustrophobia and vagueness: but to have these alone would be to have only the Hamlet of the soliloquies. In *Dipsychus* we are right inside the mind, and the duality of character does not take us very far outside. The disconcertingly narrative nature of detail and character in *Dipsychus continued* brings out clearly the functional sense of imprisonment and doubt in the first part: are there two characters or one? Not that the duality is the only extension of lyric here, there is also the sense of scene, conveyed through the varied and fluent lyric move-ments—'How pleasant it is to have money' and 'The gondola'—and having something of the local definitions of a narrative poem. There is not only the claustrophobia and doubt of this shut-in life of the tender conscience—talking to itself? to the Devil? to God?—there is also the vagueness and ambiguity of action, the threateningly half-defined rich sensual life of Italian streets and crowds, cafés and hotels, the nudges and solicitations which are just right for a poem in which sexuality is neither healthy, buoyant and joyful, as in *The Bothie*, nor weakly rational and isolated, as in *Amours de Voyage*, but menacing, coarse, violent.

III

What is the relation of intellect to passion in Clough? Walter Houghton quotes Arnold on the intellectuality of eighteenth-century poetry. 'This poetry is often eloquent, and always, in the hands of such masters as Dryden and Pope, clever; but it does not take us much below the sur-face of things, it does not give us the emotion of seeing things in their truth and beauty' and comments:

> We scarcely need to know that Clough was working within the neoclassical tradition to recognise the connection between these passages and Arnold's criticism of his poetry. For Clough's work is also too intellectual in content and method, too lacking in sensuous-ness, and therefore deficient in beauty. (*The Poetry of Clough*, New Haven and London, 1963, p. 196)

I should like to disagree with this in the strongest possible terms and insist that Clough's poetry is strongly sensuous, both in music and in visual imagery. This category of 'intellectual' poetry cannot be so simply created, by an antithesis between intellectual and sensuous. Clough's processes of analysis and argument are no more 'intellectual' if by 'intellectual' we mean 'merely or primarily intellectual', than are Donne's or Hopkins's. Houghton not only seems to accept Arnold's distinction too readily, but presses on with the case against Clough by employing Coleridge in an over-simplified fashion. Coleridge did not see imaginative poetry, as Houghton implies, as lacking in will and control: indeed, his supreme instance of imaginative art is Shakespeare, and he puts him forward as a case of art formed by will and intellect, of 'judgment equal to genius'. The confusion about Coleridge is part of a rather jumpy argument which moves from Addison to Coleridge and ends with a wrongheaded contemporary review of *Ambarvalia*. Of course Clough writes intellectual poetry, but it is poetry in which the passions and the senses are inseparable from the intellect. Clough is no more a poet in whom logic is strong and passion weak, than he is a novelist in verse. Nor would I agree that this chief gift is that of irony. Houghton is quite right to speak of his rationality, complexity, and plainness, but the heart has its reasons and its complexities, and Clough's poetry is written out of these. Clough has the rare ability to stand back from his strong passion without excess of irony. Where there is irony, it is the very rare kind that can live with strong feeling and does not shrivel it up by ridicule or criticism.

Clough never writes coldly or dryly or cynically. His poetry is compulsively argumentative but the argument is a passionate one. In it he does not pretend to be able to extricate thinking from feeling, and he is a truthful poet and a shrewd psychologist because of his inability to do so. Not only is he not a purely intellectual poet, he is not a poet in whose work thinking and feeling can be seen as even temporarily dissociated. In Donne and Marvell we can sometimes see the overlay of argument on feeling: tension can be produced by a loose relationship, a deliberately flouted argument lying loosely on the urgency of feeling, to be torn away or dropped in a climax which goes beyond or below reason. Shakespeare in the sonnets can do something similar, making a plausible argument or persuasion and then suddenly letting it go, so that a feeling is unbared—'In sleep a king, but waking no such matter'— and the intellectual equations of imagery and argument are withdrawn to show the violent caring that had been restrained up to, and only up to, this point. Such temporary and deceptive uses of argument, such sleights of ratiocination, are not to be found in Clough. He gives us in his art what he was tormented by in life, the endless impositions of thought-and-feeling which is within the experience of most average sensual intellectuals. He does occasionally separate thought and feeling in very thin layers, stripping one off the other. This is what goes on in *Dipsychus*, where layer of question is peeled off to reveal not answer but another layer of question: is this the real thing? is this the truth beneath the illusion? Is this reason just rationalisation? is the good motive a mask for greed or lust? is this doubt of the good motive a mask for cowardice or sloth?—and so on, in a persistent process of uncovering which comes to an abrupt end. The tender conscience analyses itself tenderly and conscientiously. It has to be followed, valued, and suspected because only its tenderness and conscientiousness can guide us away from coarseness and egoism, only such tenderness and conscientiousness can flatter and delude so well. We may feel impatient with the questionings and reject them as an excessive prolongation of adolescence, as an onion-peeling which we all experience and mostly have to drop because of the sheer pressure of the world's demands. In Clough's case the very conditions which toughen or kill off the tender conscience were prolonged, and not only by the energies of conscience itself. He succumbed in the end, and how unsurprising it is that he should have worked himself to death doing his official duties and helping Florence Nightingale in his spare time: tying up parcels for a good cause is the kind of activity that no tender conscience can fret to shreds, for there is no glory in it. Blanche wrote most effectively the epitaph to Clough's tender conscience:

All the new duties and interests of domestic life grew up and occupied his daily thoughts. The humour which in solitude had been inclined to take the hue of irony and sarcasm, now found its natural and healthy outlet. The practical wisdom and insight into life for which he was distinguished, were constantly exercised in the service of his friends; and the new experience which he was daily gathering at home made many perplexed questions, both social and religious, clear and simple to his mind. In this way, though he did not cease to think about the problems which hitherto had occupied his leisure, he thought about them in a different way, and was able, so to speak, to test them by the facts of actual life, and by the intuitions and experience of those whose character he valued, instead of submitting them only to the crucible of his own reflection. The close and constant contact with another mind gave him a fresh insight into his own... Having thus passed from the speculative to the constructive phase of thought, it is quite certain, from little things which he was in the habit of saying, that, had he been permitted, he would have expressed his mature convictions in works of a more positive and substantial kind. (*The Poems and Prose Remains of Arthur Hugh Clough* edited by his Wife, 2 vols., London, 1869, i, 44–5)

But it was the conscientiousness and tenderness of the tender conscience that made the poetry. It was the speculative phase in which he constructed poetry.

Speculative is just the word for Clough's poetry, as long as we see speculation as an activity of both heart and brain. It is the word to be put beside Emerson's marvellous phrase for *The Bothie*—'temperate continuity'. It is the speculative element which tempers feeling, the feeling of despair, the feeling of hope, the feeling of loss, the feeling of joy. Clough's poems never give themselves up to feeling, but neither do they distance it. The feeling warms and moves the speculation, and in fact the irony and sarcasm Blanche speaks of are very seldom there untempered. Clough is not a satirist though he very occasionally and very briefly uses pure satire, as in 'The Latest Decalogue'. A profound and sober respect for life holds him back from satire, as it held back George Eliot too. When he parodies epic in *The Bothie* he does so in no rejecting spirit. His mock-heroic has very little in common with Jane Austen's parody of the Gothic novel or with Fielding's mock-heroic: he mocks affectionately and mildly, mediates respectfully between the serious passions which form his subject and the doubt and scepticism to which he insists on exposing them. The feelings are tempered, in all senses of the word: exposed to the temperate reason, and so strengthened, not explained away but not isolated and segregated from critical thought. In *The Bothie* there is burlesque of the epic style and metre and—permitted and defined by the presence of the literary burlesque—the tempering levity to which radicalism and sensuality and their combination are exposed. There is a pervasive puncturing imagery, so often turned against the passions that the poem takes so seriously:

Other times, stung by the oestrum of some swift-working concep-
tion,
Ranged, tearing-on in his fury, an Io-cow, through the mountains,
Heedless of scenery, heedless of bogs, and of perspiration.

And there is the satire of individual characters, as in Hobbes's shot which
hits both the hero and (surely) the poem itself:

There shall he, smit by the charm of a lovely potato-uprooter
Study the question of sex in the Bothie of *What-did-he-call-it*.

It would be only three-quarters of the truth to say that such under-
minings of his study of sex and imitation of the actions of passions are
brought out in their serious intensities by the ministrations of fools
and heretics, that the way of Philip is defined by the scepticism and the
sensuality of Hobbes and the rationality of Adam. This is pretty
obviously the case, but what is also true is that Clough passes the passions through a rational filter and a tempering levity, and forces them
to meet logic, scorn and laughter. He knows only too well that one
man's grand passion is another's Io-cow. In *The Bothie* the temperate
levity is high-spirited, almost boisterous, a needed and relating spirit
for the physical rush and buoyant spurt of the central passion. It is not,
by the way, a matter of local effects: *The Bothie* creates a very elaborate
structure of feeling in which the natural landscape and sense of physicality prepare us for both the fear and the powerful celebration of sensuality towards the end, just as the levity and mock-heroics, in form
and debate, have so toughened the feelings that at the very end, in
Hobbes's letter, the poet can risk scepticism in the Rachel/Leah image.
The irony strengthens rather than undermines the final pastoral salute
to a new society, to marriage, work and fertility.

In *Amours de Voyage* the levity is placed within the central character,
and far from tempering a violent sensuality and questioning an affirmative ending, its temperate effect is undermining, and from within. The
passions are not shown in violent physicality, though as always,
Clough's presentation of sexuality is powerful and original. It is
not the naked energy of *The Bothie* or the bizarre tumescence of
'Natura Naturans' (which surely has a claim to be the most successfully sensual Victorian poem), but the tug away from and towards
sexuality:

Lo, with the rope on my loins I descend through the fissure; I
　　sink, yet
Inly secure in the strength of invisible arms up above me;
Still, wheresoever I swing, wherever to shore, or to shelf, or
Floor of cavern untrodden, shell-sprinkled, enchanting, I know I
Yet shall one time feel the strong cord tighten about me. . .

The levity of Claude is admittedly defensive, though it extends
beyond the exploration of amorous sensation and conflict, its wry mock
taking in Malthusian doctrine, 'emasculate pupils and gimcrack
churches of Iesu', his own coxcomb exultation, Parisian *millenia*, and
the British female. There are only snatches of levity, no long passages,
no concentrated satire: the wry mock is much closer to the wary feeling,
and both are seen as parts of the same temperament and mind. In
Dipsychus the tempering is perhaps most centrally and conspicuously
a part of the total form: the mocking Spirit uses mockery for his argument, and there is initially the huge gap between his crudeness and total
detachment—he *is* the satirist who flouts and inhibits feeling—and the
torturing sincerity of the tender conscience. The levity also exaggerates
sensuality and ambition and the desire for money so that we see them—
how?—either as reckless, carnal, coarse, greedy *or* as magnified and
distorted by the tender conscience. The poem unfolds and expresses
the difficulty of deciding between the sanity of laughter and its deadli-
ness. The mocking spirit is the other side of the tender conscience,
tenderness can curdle into sour rejection, and laughter can tolerate and
reject. Like E. M. Forster, Clough saw that the sense of humour can
be deadly to the feelings, and also pointed it out to an age in danger of
overvaluing humour. Yet intensities must be curbed, noonday light is
drier and truer than moonlight, and the feelings never exposed to
laughter can hardly survive. The sense of humour must not be over-
valued or undervalued.

At the heart of Clough's poetry, are the various stances, which shift,
which ask and answer, which dovetail and contradict, which may be
polarised, which may seem to mask each other, which are poles apart
or dangerously close to each other. They are most brilliantly and profoundly ordered and disordered in *Dipsychus*, which combines the
analysis of *Amours de Voyage* with the irony of *The Bothie*. There is the
contemplative mind, standing back from sexual desire, from wordly
coarseness, from ambition and greed of all kinds. It stands back in

meditation, a poet's and a scholar's meditation, studious and purely seeking. The concept of love contemplated purely, is imaginative not imaginary, ideal but not above matter:

> I hold heart can beat true to heart

and

> Love the large repose

> Restorative, not to mere outside needs
> Skin-deep, but thoroughly to the total man.

The contemplation is actual, not ideal, though hard to keep up:

> There have been times, not many, but enough
> To quiet all repinings of the heart;
> There have been times, in which my (tranquil) soul,
> No longer nebulous, sparse, errant, seemed
> Upon its axis solidly to move,
> Centred and fast; no mere chaotic blank
> For random rays to traverse unretained,
> But rounding luminous its fair ellipse
> Around its central sun.   (*Dipsychus*, Scene X)

Indeed, the sense of actuality is the important thing. His ideal is not only something within experience and experienced, but notable for its concreteness and definiteness: it affronts that feeling of thinness and unreality which accompanies contemplation out of touch with the human: and works through the solid images which are so important in this poem. The contemplation is aesthetic:

> O beautiful, beneath the magic moon,
> To walk the watery way of palaces!
> O beautiful, o'ervaulted with gemmed blue,
> This spacious court; with colour and with gold,
> With cupolas, and pinnacles, and points,
> And crosses multiplex, and tips and balls . . .

But it takes in humanity, too, and is very Wordsworthian in the movement from the inhuman to the human, 'this gay flickering crowd' and what 'seemed more profound', the sense of 'the whole mass/O' the motley facts of existence flowing by'. Then comes doubt: 'Hints haunt me ever of a More beyond', but next, instead of moving backwards towards an ideal, we suddenly and startlingly question contemplation's sufficiency, and wonder if 'what I call sin' is 'a painful opening out/of paths for ampler virtue'. Contemplation is suspected as habitual and old, 'the easy-chair of use and wont', but suspicion gives way to the suggestion that waiting may be a waiting for the ideal, for 'a necessity for God', and we move back again to the credit side of contemplation. Argument depends on feeling: we have to feel the sense of ignobility in the contemplation of the scholar and the aesthete and friends, and the sense of certainty, 'my soul secure in place,/And the vext needle perfect to her poles'. The double self is set out over and over again, in analytical terms then in detailed and close examples of opposite feelings, and last, argument shrunk and crushed to enactment, in two almost sickeningly polarised images, the one of an aimless and hopeless threading in the byways of the town, the next 'in a moment' crowning the Campanile's top, 'looking down'. This is a fine instance of the movement of poetry: the gradual narrowing from full argument, to briefer form, to images alone. The conflict and uncertainty are acted out in the structure in which we turn with no link from 'the vext needle perfect to her poles' to the next movement of the vext needle. The image of the needle is picked up indirectly in 'thread the winding byways' and the image of the pole transformed into 'the Campanile's top'. There is continuity but also a physical and imagistic swing. This is only a passage, too, in a large and elaborate pattern of variations on this oscillating movement. Dipsychus decides to accept the double life in which he is true to neither life, and the decision is expressed in an unironical religious image, in which he thinks the workday week is made bearable by the one day in seven, and must be borne for fear of losing the pure solace of that one day. This argument is taken up by the Spirit, who plays with the sabbatical image and turns it into

> Once in a fortnight say, by lucky chance
> Of happier-tempered coffee, gain (great Heaven!)
> A pious rapture: is it not enough?
> O that will keep you safe. Yet don't be sure—
> Emotions are so slippery.

The sabbatical security can be weak, cowardly, fatigued, can in the end be seduced into the wrong kind of action, end up with a chambermaid. The violent rough language of contempt and warning is set against the mild sublime of that sabbath peace, and 'Emotions are so slippery' is another instance of this argument in feeling: the Spirit argues but uses sarcasm, laughter, contempt, and to Dipsychus whose vacillations of image have already shown the slipperiness. This is the best against the worst, but the relationships are complex, and we move to the lowest point from the highest through several swings and shifts. 'The lowest point': the formulation just cannot be made in these terms. Dipsychus is not Marlowe's Faust, and he only resembles Goethe's insofar as his final 'redemption' is made possibly co-terminous with his fall. Is the lowest point the highest after all? The Spirit points out to Dipsychus that just as the Devil can quote Scripture so God can masquerade and use the Devil. But it is the Spirit that says so. Dipsychus tells the Spirit that he is crudely misled in thinking such pacts are binding, but Marlowe's Faust said something similarly brash in 'I think hell's a fable'. The suggestions are resonant, but made by powerful interests which twist and modify, so that we do not know: 'Perhaps he wasn't a devil after all. That's the beauty of the poem; nobody can say'. We see the possibilities vibrate, as relativism and interest undermine assertion, and we do not even know whether to express doubt in God's name or in the Devil's. Clough is too impassioned and too uncertain to be praised as an ironist. To call him an 'intellectual' poet is as misleading as to call him a verse-novelist. He is a feeling analyst, a writer of lyrical narrative, an ironist who moves beyond irony, an intellectual both sensuous and passionate.

Belief and unbelief are accommodated in the scepticism *and* in the hopefulness at the end of *Dipsychus*: it may be easier to see the defeat of the Devil (if he is one) if belief is admitted or flouted. If you lost or kept faith the habit of self-scrutiny made its pressure felt, especially at Arnold's Rugby—though we must observe Clough's warning to his uncle in the Epilogue, 'You must not refer it to Arnold, at all at all' and 'I ascribe it to the spirit of the time. The real cause of the evil you complain of . . . was, I take it, the religious movement of the last century, beginning with Wesleyanism, and culminating at last in Puseyism. This over-excitation of the religious sense, resulting in this irrational, almost animal irritability of conscience, was, in many ways, as foreign to Arnold as it is proper to—'. Characteristically, the sentence is left unfinished as his uncle's levity interrupts. Clough's argument here is also a declaration of bias and interest. The tenderness of conscience was of course not just a matter of the over-excitation of the religious sense, with the special difficulties of the humanist's ethic which faced the ex-Christian. It is also a function of sexual problems: Philip's problems and Claude's and Dipsychus's and Clough's. Sexual choice and conflict in and out of marriage both seemed and was different. Clough's anguished discriminations between a 'bestial' love which he recognises in 'Love and Reason' as still better than beastly for being human, a love which can enlist Reason on its side, and a love 'that itself was Reason' have the special cutting edge of his own time, without being entirely blunted a century later. The problem of work and money was also a pointedly Victorian one: Clough had to choose first between a conscienceless financial security in Oxford and an honest hand-to-mouth existence after he gave up his fellowship. Then he had the choice between an uncommitted freelance insecurity as a celibate and a dull office job in order to keep a wife. Religion and economics and sex wove a complex web for Clough: the tender and over-excited conscience had real enough problems. The poetry is not only the deeply moving record of intelligent passion but a document of its time, capable of considerable detachment but, as I see it, never losing the attachment to the personal.

4

Forms and Feelings in the Sonnets of Gerard Manley Hopkins

There has been so much discussion and exegesis of Hopkins's knowledge, belief and thought that we can perhaps now take them for granted in order to look harder at their relation to the poetic passions. Passion in Hopkins is highly individual, and one vital aspect of his poetry is his command of an intense passionate distinctness in part and whole.

Lyric poetry frequently cuts out history and character entirely: Hopkins's poetry invariably does, with the exception of 'The Wreck of the Deutschland'. It rather less frequently cuts out moral judgment: Hopkins is indeed a lyric poet whose values are constantly and intimately blended with his passions. But the action of judgment depends on the action of passion, and forms part of that action. Judgments in poetry are passionate acts. Hopkins's poetry is concerned with strong feelings of hope, praise, faith, patience, desire—the changing expressions on the face of love. It is also concerned with love's negative feelings of dullness, loss, torment, fear, antagonism, dryness, anger, even the approaches to despair. In Hopkins the poetic forms of feeling are evaluative; the passions are judged as they are uttered. The poetry of rapture is proud of its celebration and pleased with its praise. The agonised verse fights against dryness or despair, learns to value friction, loss, or a small-scale relief. Judgment of passion creates its own tensions and intensities: confidence heightens admiration, judgment and analysis confirm humiliation. The chaff flies in the agonised winnowing. Passion judges and analyses passion.

Lyric poetry can also be free, if it chooses, from the need or tendency to classify and name its passions, and though Hopkins is a poet who does a good deal of naming of feeling, the advantage I speak of is strongly his possession. D. H. Lawrence tells us that the naming of feeling is deceptively lucid: it is in danger of falsifying the nature of passion and impeding our knowledge of our hearts. Suzanne Langer, in *Philosophy in a New Key*, speaks with sympathy of the view that music expresses 'the composer's *knowledge* of human feeling': the lyric poet may be more committed to naming than the composer but has something of his ability to explore and enact the complexity and fluidity of feeling. Too much naming simplifies the complexity and puts a frame round the flux.

Hopkins names feelings, but leaves their complex action unimpeded by the action of naming. 'My own heart let me more have pity on', he says, in a poem which relates aspects of giving, taking, needing, waiting and believing in pity of various kinds, inner and outer. 'To my sad self hereafter kind', he says in the same poem, which also presents the action of wanting kindness and creating a context for kindness, of feeling sadness, tolerating it, and trying to change it. He names patience, in a poem which is an extraordinary expression and enactment of the changing need for patience, the hardness and gentleness of patience. 'Glory be to God for dappled things', he begins; 'Praise him' he ends. The relation between beginning and ending in this poem might be described as the movement through particularities to simplicity, the earning of understanding, clarity, and love. 'Carrion Comfort' names and defines Despair but its action marks the hideous nearness and the vital distance; a distance moving, changing, alive with possibilities of loss and gain. 'No worst, there is none' names grief, world-sorrow, fury, and struggles up, like a Beckett story, along a tiny but terribly difficult track from torment to a small-scale respite, 'a comfort serves in a whirlwind'. In all these poems the naming is so plainly only a part of the whole enactment, and so plainly differentiated from enactment, that it draws attention to the complex and elusive flux of the unnameable. The struggle or drama or structure of feeling contains and transcends the fixities and definites of naming.

Some of the poems name several feelings; some refrain from naming; some postpone naming so that the coming of the name is part of the dénouement or consummation. I want to suggest, in passing, that there are some instances where the form and the feeling fail, where instead of feeling an expansion or a movement towards a climax or a whole track of complex passion, we feel let down or reduced or restricted. Instances of such reduction of feeling are, 'In the Valley of the Elwy' and—alas—'Spring'. In each case we begin with a powerful, passionate, and sensuous rendering; in the 'Valley' of a tender cordiality in men and nature, in 'Spring' of painfully fresh and delicate rapture. Instead of a movement into a larger recognition that discards nothing of the sensuous or human, we then turn into the reduction of allegory, of dogma, of message. Such poems, happily few and far between, constrict the more than usual state of emotion into an inappropriate order. The part asserts itself at the expense of the whole. Something is left out and lost.

More native to the poetry of Hopkins is the process of expansion, in which we move from one stage of feeling to another, usually from the sensuous and phenomenal to the larger spiritual adventure. In such poems the initial states or stages of feeling are transcended but not obliterated. One of the simplest instances is 'Pied Beauty'.

> Glory be to God for dappled things—
>   For skies of couple-colour as a brinded cow;
>   For rose-moles all in stipple upon trout that swim;
> Fresh-firecoal chestnut-falls; finches' wings;
>   Landscape plotted and pieced—fold, fallow, and plough;
>   And áll trádes, their gear and tackle and trim.
>
> All things counter, original, spare, strange;
>   Whatever is fickle, freckled (who knows how?)
>   With swift, slow; sweet, sour; adazzle, dim;
> He fathers-forth whose beauty is past change:
>   Praise him.

The sonnet has a smooth and lucid track of feeling. The poet goes from the celebration of joy, delight, admiration and love for the variety of natural and man-made creation ('no art but nature makes that art') to the simple praise of the single source. The process is smooth but each stage has its intricacy. We begin with exhilarated utterance. 'Glory be to God for dappled things', and this is explicit, reverent, and attached to devotional and colloquial tradition. We proceed through a series of listed attentive praises, each of which is part of a lucid demonstration of variety in unity and a sensitive exclamation of delight. The very act of accumulation is itself exciting, in its implications of piled-up abundance and its delighted clamour: 'this and this and this', it says, or rather, to be precise, 'this *and* this and *this!*'; but accumulation is not the only end, and the complex structure shows precisely what Coleridge meant by distinct gratification from the component parts, and a gratification serving the end of the whole poem.

Each spurt of appreciation uses fresh terms of aesthetic value: 'colour', 'rose', 'fresh', 'counter, original, spare, strange'; but the general evaluative terms are part of a highly sensitive account of the particulars: 'skies of couple-colour as a brinded cow' and 'rose-moles all in stipple upon trout that swim' and 'Fresh-firecoal chestnut-falls'. The acute sensitivity shows in two ways: the sensuous range of texture, colour, feel, taste, pattern, and in the startling conjunction of two kinds of dappled thing in the first three instances. The pied beauty of skies is described through the simile of the pied beauty of the cow; the pied beauty of the trout through the pied beauty of the compound 'rose-moles', the pied beauty of the chestnut-fall in terms of the pied beauty of fire and coal and the compound 'Fresh-firecoal'. There is opposition and wide contrast: the sky and the cow; the rose and the trout; the fire *and* the chestnut. We are made to feel the variety of the phenomenal world within *and* the variety of each phenomenon. All this in a way which cannot be fixed by generalisation: in each of these three instances there is a different kind of coupling. After the series has been set off, in a way which makes the existence of the series itself plain but present in vivid particulars, the poet is free to pluralise and generalise less particularly: 'Landscape plotted and pieced—fold, fallow, and plough;/ And áll trádes, their gear and tackle and trim'. Next, even more reductively, come twelve adjectives, also set out in series but variedly: four synonyms; 'counter, original, spare, strange'; then two, 'fickle, freckled', one drawn from a highly conceptual and one from a very physical field; and then the three sets of opposites, 'swift, slow' and so on. The poem then concludes with two utterly simple lines where neither subject, image nor language is dappled or pied. The conclusion is uttered directly and explicitly, and in the brief last line of two words, in a ritual and traditional language, which turns its back on all idiosyncrasy: 'Praise him'. The poem has taken us through a highly eccentric and particularised utterance to a final abnegation of variety. But the final praise depends on the experience of variety. There is a reasoned praise of the individuality and variety which is then reduced, removed, pared-down, and finally comprehended. The poem accumulates, discovers, and finally arrives at oneness; its passage is from 'Glory be to God for dappled things' to 'Praise him'. It makes us *know* Hopkins's knowledge of praise and worship.

There are many longer journeys and greater distances in these short poems. 'Pied Beauty' is a useful beginning because of its relatively simple and short action, but also because of its quirkiness of detail. Not only knowledge, thought, and belief, but also the extreme idiosyncrasy of Hopkins's poetry can make it hard to follow its passions. Its peculiarity, its oddness, and its celebration and discussion of peculiarity and oddness, may distract the attention from what is of course individual but less idiosyncratic as poetic achievement. What Hopkins says about Purcell in that great sonnet 'Henry Purcell' is apposite here. The poet knows that what Purcell is after is 'mood' and 'meaning, proud fire or sacred fear/ Or love or pity' but admits that this is not what he as listener responds to: 'It is the forgèd feature finds me; it is the rehearsal / Of own, of abrúpt sélf there so thrusts on, so throngs the ear'. The splendid though self-admittedly obscure image at the end says the same thing: the great stormfowl is concerned with motion—'but meaning motion'—but the act of soaring catches us with the individuality, the 'sakes', 'quaint moonmarks ... pelted plumage under/ Wings'. The subject and form of inscape in Hopkins has naturally occupied our attention to the exclusion of those features he shares with all great lyric poets. But Hopkins himself knew that the individualising marks were in some respects incidental. That is how I interpret his comment on this poem, in his explanatory letter to Bridges of 26 May 1897.

> The thought is that as the seabird opening his wings with a whiff of wind in your face means the whirr of the motion, but also unaware gives you a whiff of knowledge about his plumage, the marking of which stamps his species, that he does not mean, so Purcell, seemingly intent only on the thought or feeling he is to express or call out, incidentally lets you remark the individualising marks of his own genius.

There is no point, however, in arguing about the relative importance of the individualising mark and the typical action of feeling, not least because while the centrality of enacted feeling is common to all lyric poets, it is in each poem given a unique utterance. That is the point: when we name and categorise love and pity and fear and despair we mean and say much the same kind of thing. But each poem gives an individual experience of feeling.

We have seen one track or trajectory of feeling in 'Pied Beauty'. One thing that poem shows is the special relation of the part and the whole. The 'parts'—sentences, stages, images, instances, items in a series, were vivid: the poem's action of praise and celebration depended on a vivid and checkered sense of what was praised, but there were stages and degrees in that vividness, an ordered movement from greater to less particularity. This kind of movement through variety to singleness, in an action of celebration, is present in several of the nature sonnets: it is the characteristic form or the theme of inscape, though presented not as unparticularised idea, belief of fact but as idea, belief and fact mobilised in the sensuous, reasoning and active forms of feeling. If we take several of the nature-sonnets, the fact or belief or idea is common ground, but the movement of feeling is always individual. In 'Hurrahing in Harvest', for instance, a summary statement of subject, and even of imagery, can sound very like the statement of subject imagery in 'Pied Beauty' or 'The Starlight Night'. But the life of feeling is unique.

Summer ends now; now, barbarous in beauty, the stooks rise
   Around; up above, what wind-walks! what lovely behaviour
   Of silk-sack clouds! has wilder, wilful-wavier
Meal-drift moulded ever and melted across skies?

I walk, I lift up, I lift up heart, eyes,
   Down all that glory in the heavens to glean our Saviour;
   And, éyes, heárt, what looks, what lips yet gave you a
Rapturous love's greeting of realer, of rounder replies?

And the azurous hung hills are his world-wielding shoulder
   Majestic—as a stallion stalwart, very-violet-sweet!—
These things, these things were here and but the beholder
   Wanting; which two when they once meet,
The heart réars wíngs bold and bolder
   And hurls for him, O half hurls earth for him off under his feet.

There is the accumulation and appreciation of the sensuous particulars, the delighted praise of varied beauty, and the ultimate climax in a greater delight and praise. There is the characteristic oddity and variety in the compounds, creations, and yokings of image: 'wind-walks', 'wilful-wavier/Meal-drift' and of course, 'as a stallion stalwart, very-violet-sweet!' But if we take in not only the theme and imagery of inscapes and instress, the variety and unity, but the structure of feeling, it becomes apparent that this is an individual experience of sensation and passion. In 'Pied Beauty' we felt loving appreciation and wonder at variety giving way, solemn and awed and simple-seeing, to the sense of unity. This is a passionate action composed of very different feelings and of feeling differently ordered. Here the sensations that begin the poem are those of the roughness and violence of the end of summer: the beauty of the stooks is 'barbarous', the word economically blends the rough feeling and look of the harvest with the precisely made pun on 'beard'. The roughness of the ground is reflected in the windy motions of the sky. Moreover, the initial rapturous feeling about this roughness is followed at once by the movement and vision. 'I walk, I lift up, I lift up heart, eyes' and 'what lips yet gave you a/Rapturous love's greeting of realer, of rounder replies?' We then swerve back again, in a zig-zag motion, to the hills, another type of something grand and passionate. The movement of the lines is also abrupt and exclamatory, and so is certainly the structure of the central image which takes us from the stallion to the violet. The last three lines are hard and vigorous both in what they say and how they say it, especially in the last line, which has a break and lift in its middle, 'And hurls for him, O half hurls earth for him off under his feet'. Our feet are abruptly displaced here too. Both in imagery and structure the feeling is boisterous: the formal analogy would be no smooth curve but a zig-zag. The individual structure of feeling is produced by emphasis and repetition, exclamation and interruption. It is a poem of boisterous rapture, not calm of discovery, and its form is appropriate.

'Pied Beauty' and 'Hurrahing in Harvest' are love-poems, as Hopkins knew. He said that the poetic impulse was strong feeling, usually love; and we could say of his verse, as of the love-poetry of Donne, that it works out many different experiences and aspects of love. There is a very common movement, towards recovery, meaning, affirmation and triumph; though it is by no means invariable. But even where it is present, it is given different rhythms and movements in different poems.

As a dare-gale skylark scanted in a dull cage
   Man's mounting spirit in his bone-house, mean house, dwells—
   That bird beyond the remembering his free fells;
This in drudgery, day-labouring-out life's age.
Though aloft on turf or perch or poor low stage,
   Both sing sometímes the sweetest, sweetest spells,
   Yet both droop deadly sómetimes in their cells
Or wring their barriers in bursts of fear or rage.

Not that the sweet-fowl, song-fowl, needs no rest—
Why, hear him, hear him babble and drop down to his nest,
   But his own nest, wild nest, no prison.

Man's spirit will be flesh-bound when found at best,
But uncumberèd: meadow-down is not distressed
   For a rainbow footing it nor he for his bónes rísen.

The poem begins with a quatrain which has a downward movement, in cadence, sentence-pattern, stanza-pattern, and imagery: each line except the fourth begins high and ends low. We move, for instance, from 'dare-gale' to 'dull cage' and from 'mounting spirit' to 'bone-house, mean house'. Then comes an apparent recovery in the second quatrain: after all, there is song in the cage, but the sense of joy and relief drops into frustration and sadness. The first tercet begins an upward movement, both in the line and the whole stanza, and lifts us in a gentle preparation for the flight of the last tercet, with its tremendous image and movement of release, its unencumbered lift and flight. The great final image is a triumph of Hopkins's sensuous and symbolic imagining: 'meadow-down is not distressed/For a rainbow footing it nor he for his bónes rísen'. Here there is not only a haunting cadence, inseparable from the effect of the sense of enlargement in 'nor he for his bónes rísen' but a precisely imagined tactual image. It is precise because we accept at once the softness of the rainbow footing—the image of something seen and yet unseen, something physical and yet elusive and intangible. The rainbow comes and goes, we never see where it ends, we cannot touch it. This image joins with the equally delicate ambiguity of 'meadow-down' where the softness of the feather (down) and the grass (downy) merges with the gentle meadow-slope (down). It is perhaps most astonishing that such sense of almost ineffable physicality is felt before the traditional associations of the Covenant. The feeling of the extraordinary triumph of a body resurrected depends on this feat of the phenomenal and symbolic imagination. But the breathtaking climax depends on the whole poetic proceeding; though the eloquent image, whose dimension of beauty is part of its value, is felt as climactic, it is an impressive part of a brilliant whole. Each stage and step makes us aware of height and depth, and in a locally particularised way: each movement has contributed to the final lift and proof of faith. There was the sense of the lifted song, even in the cage; then the sense of a drop, but after all to a nest, not a prison; and finally to the 'interpretation' which does not reduce or abstract the other imaged and structured heights and depths, but depends on their structure and resonance and completes their sensational power. Here is argument, idea, belief, fact, dissolved and realised in the form of mobile and complex feeling: constraint, dullness, longing, nostalgia, oppression, grind, relief, rage and fear, limited hope, consolation in a small way, then larger hope, height, expansion, assured and joyful vision related to the phenomenal world but soaring beyond it.

This poem is one of the poet's most subtle and lovely achievements, and one of its explicit statements can speak for his own poetic range: from 'sweetest, sweetest spells' to 'bursts of fear or rage'. In the sonnets that deal with the dark and bitter passions we have a process very like that of the triumphant sonnets of praise, but telling a very different tale of feeling. Here too we are given the powerful expression of naked feeling, unnamed, unexplained, unpersonalised, though not unjudged. There is no story, no character, but the action and structure of the passions. We could extract or generalise from several poems the theme of deprivation and love, loss of faith and hope, agony and a little respite, but the detail of each sonnet is its own. The whole point of this poetry is its passionate particularity.

> My own heart let me more have pity on; let
> Me live to my sad self hereafter kind,
> Charitable; not live this tormented mind
> With this tormented mind tormenting yet.
>   I cast for comfort I can no more get
> By groping round my comfortless, than blind
> Eyes in their dark can day or thirst can find
> Thirst's all-in-all in all a world of wet.
>
> Soul, self; come, poor Jackself, I do advise
> You, jaded, let be; call off thoughts awhile
> Elsewhere; leave comfort root-room; let joy size
> At God knows when to God knows what; whose smile
> 's not wrung, see you; unforeseen times rather—as skies
> Betweenpie mountains—lights a lovely mile.

In the first deceptively and yet appropriately quiet line there is the naming of pity, but in an explicit statement of intent and need which is almost at once overtaken and answered by the action of feeling. The poem says that kindness and pity are necessary, and starts showing that it is hard, though necessary, to do something for oneself and also to wait for something to come from beyond self. It is rather like acting out this theme: 'My own heart let me more have pity on' qualified thus, 'And it is not as easy as all that to translate intent into action'. The poem is a very fine instance of passional action breaking down and commenting on simple and rigid and naming of passion. This poetry is about the inadequacy of giving names to the feelings.

Even this puts the matter too simply. The contrast is not just between talking about the feelings and feeling, but between talking about them in a particular way and feeling them in more complexity and fluidity. In the first two lines of 'My own heart' we have a strikingly slow and hesitant motion, marked by a characteristic use of experimental and maximal stress. We have all as children played with permutations of stress, discovering the flexibility and variety of the English sentence, trying to shift stress from one word to another and perhaps trying to put as much stress on every word in a sentence as the sentence can stand. The first line seems to begin with the stress on 'own' and 'heart' and then perhaps on 'let' and 'more' and 'pity' too; and the same exploration of stress is repeated in the next line, where there is not only the tentative shift, from 'live' to 'sad' and 'self' but the sense of verbal replacement too; perhaps it is not a case of more having pity on the heart but being kind to the larger 'sad self', and in the next two lines the replacement is even more striking, as we replace the self which has replaced the heart with the mind. If we thought this was a sorting-out or a movement towards clarity and singleness, like the process of 'Pied Beauty', we should be very wrong, for the whole conceptual drama has been re-christened: this is about stopping the torment of mind by mind. The poem begins by dramatising the pained bewilderment of finding out exactly what is wrong and who is doing what to whom and what can be done or not done about it.

I need not labour the local dramatisations of feeling in the vicious circle of the 'this tormented mind/With this tormented mind tormenting yet' where circularity, closure, tension and repetition are violently expressive. In the second quatrain there is the local pattern of feeling in the abrupt and functional 'failure' of 'comfortless'. Next comes a typically powerful break in a series: 'blind/Eyes in their dark' are not to 'day' as 'thirst' is to 'thirst's all-in-all', and the difference marks the movement out of the enclosure, towards at least the recognition of hope. Between the initial statement, in itself both a generalisation and a kind action, and the final comforting address and performance of love in the second part of the sonnet, is an intricate movement of feeling: the passional action between the two moments has been frustrating, frustrated, advancing a little, slightly relieved, fatigued, opening and relaxing with an effort. This account of the movement of feeling scarcely glances at the implications of imagery, but of course the structure cannot be separated from the image-associations. The action of the first and final moments seems to be summed up in the images: they show the process of being kind to yourself, of needing kindness, of finding it hard to give or take kindness; it shows what is meant by leaving comfort root-room and so on, and finally when we reach the image of God's smile like light shining through hills, we have come through the impassioned journey from dark to light. Almost every image could be tested and analysed thus, as a microcosm of the structure of feeling. This structure, incidentally, shows how Hopkins exploits the sonnet-form, how he knows everything about its capacity for concentration, turn, climax, and summary but also how stunningly he grasps its flexibility. He can be taken as a model sonneteer, but is very far from being model-bound. In fact he shows up the abstractness and crudeness of talking about concentration, turn, climax and all that.

> Patience, hard thing! the hard thing but to pray,
> But bid for, Patience is! Patience who asks
> Wants war, wants wounds; weary his times, his tasks;
> To do without, take tosses, and obey.
>   Rare patience roots in these, and, these away,
> Nowhere. Natural heart's ivy, Patience masks
> Our ruins of wrecked past purpose. There she basks
> Purple eyes and seas of liquid leaves all day.
>
>   We hear our hearts grate on themselves: it kills
> To bruise them dearer. Yet the rebellious wills
> Of us we do bid God bend to him even so.
>   And where is he who more and more distils
> Delicious kindness?—He is patient. Patience fills
> His crisp combs, and that comes those ways we know.

Here is a new passional drama. I use the word 'drama' to point to the tremendous activity in the poem. 'My own heart' had action and *personae* (I, heart, self, mind, God) but here there are only the two characters[1] on the bare stage, the human being and God. I want to emphasise the movement and structure of the 'drama'. 'Patience' does not move by inching forward and back, taking two forward steps and one backward step, like 'My own heart' but constantly and inexorably advances. Yet it too has patterns of repetition and circularity. It is indeed an appropriately circular structure, while 'My own heart' eventually makes an advance and stays with it. In 'Patience' we move to the climactic image of the honey, with its associations of sweetness and colour, golden generosity, softness, nourishment and healing lubrication. We then move away, referred back terribly to the whole past of the poem-up-to-now in, 'that comes those ways we know'. The end is very hard in this return to the beginning, but makes its inevitable proposal gravely, sagely, soberly, with the sense of a full experience and knowledge of Patience. The responsiveness of the image of honey to the earlier terrible physicality of 'We hear our hearts grate on themselves' shows once against Hopkins's sensational range and power, in physical instance and symbol. The hearts that 'grate on themselves 'are an extraordinary feat of metaphor. The 'argument' depends on the ambiguous plurality of 'our hearts', which literally refers to our human collective possession of more than one heart, but allows him to convey the horrible tactile idea of a physical heart grating against or on itself. Like—though also unlike—the rainbow of the resurrection this is a kind of image of the unimaginable, in its ambiguity, its physical and conceptual merging, and its horror of feeling what should never be felt (like the pleura-shock described in *The Magic Mountain*). After such abrasion, the honey is a needed healing. But the responsive image also suggests a store for future needs, and therefore future friction: it is honey stored in the comb. Lastly, it stands for God's patience as well as ours, and this is the new point made in the poem's final magnificent expansion. It really has a double climax and surprise: Patience never ends, its need continues, so back to the beginning; and, Patience is not only a gift of God but something he must also need, given the human creature. The poem proves what is meant by 'dearer' in 'it kills/To bruise them dearer' by

---

[1] This is of course to ignore the drama of image and personification which so often creates a kind of inner-stage drama, a play within the play, in Hopkins's sonnets, and to discuss this one would have to include blind Eyes, Dark, Day, Thirst, Patience, and so on.

5

Passion and Contemplation in Yeats's Love Poetry

Passion, Yeats said, is contemplation, that is, an imaginative experience. Poetic passion has to be contemplative, for the pulse and play of bodies defy poetic expression; even passions outside poetry usually comprehend the brooding of anticipation and aftermath. Thwarted passions bring their special forms of introspection, which postulate or remember images of action in desperation or patience. The ardent meditations of Yeats's love lyrics create and cherish images of love, in praise, memory, and yearning. The impulse to make and inspect images of love cannot be pure sentiment, but the ideology and mythology of Yeats's images have been so well scrutinised that it is perhaps a relief to insist on the forms of feeling in particular poems.

Like the daw who first builds and then broods over her wild nest in 'The Tower', Yeats is concerned with making and contemplating his images of experience. All poetry is about itself, or at least about the imagination that makes it: Yeats's love lyrics are not only introspections, but also movements of will and feeling. His poetry propounds admiration, desire, affection, and fidelity. It seems frequently possessive, or impelled by possessiveness. It is particularly good at rendering affinity and closeness. In 'A Bronze Head' he speaks of a 'propinquity' which 'brought/Imagination to that pitch where it casts out/All that is not itself', and one could go a lot further and find no better definition of imagination and love. Yeats's love poetry, like Shakespeare's and Donne's, so contemplates passion as to give us new knowledge of the passions.

A mingling of possessiveness and praise is present in an early poem, placid, elegant, romantic, vague, and at first sight far removed from the violence and stridency of the Crazy Jane poems or 'The Three Bushes'. 'The Lover Tells of the Rose in his Heart' (*The Wind Among the Reeds*, 1899) is not static in its contemplation, though what it eventually

works towards seems to be an enclosure of the image of love,
secure and private. Undesirable or incompatible experiences are set up,
rather faintly and feebly to occupy nearly the whole poem, taking a
long time to be eliminated, suspending the climax, and suggesting the
indispensability of their presences:

> All things uncomely and broken, all things worn out and old,
> The cry of a child by the roadway, the creak of a lumbering cart,
> The heavy steps of the ploughman, splashing the wintry mould,
> Are wronging your image that blossoms a rose in the deeps of
>   my heart.
>
> The wrong of unshapely things is a wrong too great to be told;
> I hunger to build them anew and sit on a green knoll apart,
> With the earth and the sky and the water, remade, like a casket
>   of gold
> For my dreams of your image that blossoms a rose in the deeps
>   of my heart.

Almost every discarded item here is to recur as an essential aspect of
love, defiantly or shockingly acclaimed, in the later love poetry. Crazy
Jane's body is a road men have passed over, she makes love on grass
and in ditches, the poet lies down in the foul rag-and-bone shop,
nothing can be whole that is not rent, and love pitches its tent in the
place of excrement. Age may give a new urgency, desperation, hysteria, and even ugliness to sexual passion, its desecrations violating
aesthetic and romantic charms of sex to assert a new purity. The young
Yeats could hardly be expected to forecast that, though perhaps there
are signs of anticipation in 'The Lamentation of the Old Pensioner'.
If the roebuck in 'The Indian upon God' tends to be languid, 'so sad and
soft, a gentle thing like me', there is a touch of erotic hysteria when the
poet resents the amorous cries of beast and bird in 'He Thinks of his
Past Greatness When a Part of the Constellation of Heaven'.

In 'The Lover Tells of the Rose in his Heart', the unlovely and broken
things lack individual force, but press hard, and accumulate pressure.
Love's imaged rose cannot be contemplated without their dismissal,
and the poem moves in a process of rejection, impatiently and dis-
approvingly removing or transforming things in order to make an
appropriate recess for love. The rose is remote, sacred, and private, and
it takes some effort to find it a proper sanctuary. That effort provides

all the vitality the poem possesses. It is not easy to work out a clear image of its construction of containers and contents: the syntax of the last line, with all the pressure of slow dismissal behind it, seems to push further and further away from the outside into depths, 'like a casket of gold/For my dreams of your image that blossoms a rose in the deeps of my heart'. The pressure works to its end, though the order is dislocated, for the rose appears halfway through the last line, not at the end. The image presumably becomes a rose in his dreams, and those dreams are presumably enclosed in the deeps of his heart, which is in its turn enclosed in the strenuously wrought casket. A momentary sense of noble impulse seems to stir as he hungers to rebuild the unshapely things, but it is not so much a new earth he wants as a suitably enclosed and excellent treasure-box.

The poem is conceited but not witty, inviting irony or even ridicule in its preciousness of intent, but it has a certain plaintive charm and energy. The desire to cherish the image is perfectly intelligible, suggestive of the early auto-erotic fantasies of Sligo, as well as Maud Gonne's encouragement of a romantic and idealistic image-making love. The poem usefully describes itself, and the larger poetic enterprise of which it is only a part, through the attempt to replace an awkwardly huge and various nature with something fine, skilfully wrought and manageable, like a casket. It also draws attention to the poetic and amorous inclination to praise, preserve, and brood rather privately over what has been made. It clearly refers to more than erotic poetry and purpose, and Yeats's interest in condensing experience into images at once abstractedly lucid and sensuously particular is of course not confined to love poetry. The casket looks ahead to the gold and enamel singing-birds of Byzantium. 'The Tower' and 'The Circus Animals' Desertion' are both concerned with the artist's problematic creation of images which will elucidate experience without falsifying it. Such questions, while not confined to amorous verses, happen to show themselves there with convenient plainness.

Yeats disliked the moralising, describing, and narrating which loomed so large in Victorian poetry, and made special efforts to cut down and condense experience, as all lyric poets must, in the intense contemplation of moods and moments. The making of images is one way of securing such compression and distillation. Yeats sometimes achieves his selections from narration and description in a very small compass indeed. There is a group of short lyric declarations, beginning

in *The Wind Among the Reeds* (1899) and continuing into *The Tower*
(1928), which show his capacity for implication and generalisation.
The first impression made by these poems is that of a simplicity,
directness, and conversational looseness, whose concentration is not
immediately apparent. The earliest example, 'The Lover Mourns for
the Loss of Love', can stand as a type of the unassuming, elastic form.
It has a typical iambic tendency, an informal flow, and consists of a
single sentence less artless than it first seems:

> Pale brows, still hands and dim hair,
> I had a beautiful friend
> And dreamed that the old despair
> Would end in love in the end:
> She looked in my heart one day
> And saw your image was there;
> She has gone weeping away.

    The poem begins with a fairly specific description of one woman
(Olivia Shakespear), particularised in what Pound calls the 'excessive
chevelure' and Ellmann[1] the 'pallor, dimness, and whiteness' and
'generalised look of a Burne-Jones figure', typical of the amorous
poems of this period. There is a marked contrast between this portrait,
which is full, if vague, and the image of the other woman (Maud
Gonne), which offers no particulars but is simply 'your image'.
Although the poem is direct compared with 'The Lover Tells of the
Rose in His Heart', it also tells of a dismissal and a recall. The new
love's departure effectively proves and praises the security and constancy of the heart's casket where the image is kept, on this occasion
not too privately or invisibly. There is some narrative implicit, in the
mention of despair and hope, but the emotions are activated as well as
recounted. Because the new mistress had begun to replace despair by
hope, her departure is a sad business for the poet as well as for her.
The fourth line, 'Would end in love in the end', is suitably dull and
hollow, the misery spreading over the old despair, the transient hope,
and the new sorrow. It is perhaps a self-indulgent, or a Maud-
indulging, poem, for the final plaintiveness cannot be quite allowed its
full weight, contradicted as it is by the complacent triumph of old
memory. Maud Gonne's image has won, and the poem is not so
complex as to be able to make a space for both the victory and the loss.

[1] Richard Ellmann, *The Identity of Yeats* (London, 1954), ch. 2.

The other poems in the group include 'The Lover Pleads with his Friend for Old Friends' (also in *The Wind Among the Reeds*), 'A Deep-Sworn Vow', and 'Memory' (both in *The Wild Swans at Coole*, 1919), and two poems on related but different subjects, scarcely touching Maud's image, 'After Long Silence' (*Words for Music Perhaps and Other Poems*, 1932), and 'The New Faces' (*The Tower*, 1929). The first three are all concerned with Maud Gonne's image, faithfully and defiantly preserved. Each of the poems, too, recounts a single event like the dismissal of the new friend by the old. In 'The Lover Pleads with his Friend for Old Friends' the poet argues that despite *her* new friends, her imaged beauty will be most effectively preserved for and by his eyes. The story is that of fidelity, but makes a poetic, as well as an amorous, claim. The parenthesis of the second and third lines is hostile enough to reflect ironically on her 'shining'. It is a brilliantly jealous poem:

> Though you are in your shining days,
> Voices among the crowd
> And new friends busy with your praise,
> Be not unkind or proud,
> But think about old friends the most:
> Time's bitter flood will rise,
> Your beauty perish and be lost
> For all eyes but these eyes.

In 'A Deep-Sworn Vow' her image is not all there is in his life, which because of her broken vow, needs other friendships but is so deeply imprinted as to return, with thoughts of death, and with sleep and wine. In 'Memory', one of the most beautiful of his love poems, no other image can last because hers has so embedded itself as to have permanently changed his shape. Once more he retains her image, not in a casket but in the body's memory. 'The Lover Pleads with his Friend for Old Friends' speaks of 'shining days' and of her 'beauty', but none of these poems is visually specific about the image. 'A Deep-Sworn Vow' goes into some detail about the new images while keeping quiet about 'your face'. All the poems consider the imagination of love.

Conclusion and climax, which usually coincide, make the under-statement ring out. In a preface to *A Selection from the Poetry of W. B. Yeats* (1913) Yeats speaks of the aid given by elocution or music to form, 'it is speaking or singing before an audience that makes us tell our stories well, and put our thoughts into some lasting order and set our emotions clambering to some arduous climax. . .' The arduous clamber is evident in these poems, even though the distances are bounded. There is a sense of an alp being scaled. The pressure of implicit narrative is considerable. What the compressed or buried story tells is what the feeling mounts towards, and triumphantly reaches in a final assertion of constancy. The image is flourished, his possession asserted, and the beloved praised. Olivia Shakespear's melancholy departure faintly trails away after the affirmation of the constant image in a properly if valedictory fashion, but the other endings strongly affirm the image, 'Suddenly I see your face', 'For no eyes but these eyes', and 'Where the mountain hare has lain'. After the first poem, there is really no other image to compete with hers.

In *The Identity of Yeats* Richard Ellmann remarks that *The Wind Among the Reeds* repeats 'a small number of words . . . again and again, as if the poet wished to confine himself to a small nook of the language'. This restriction and repetition play a positive role in the brief declarations of fidelity. I have already noted the line, 'Would end in love in the end', where the slight awkwardness seems honestly embarrassed, almost stammering, suggesting that there is no time or space for elegant variation or the avoidance of repetition. Maternal brooding, in birds or humans, often involves an intensely loving murmur, and its affectionate repetitions of words or sounds are mimicked in Yeats, often with erotic effect. Each repetition has an individual function. 'All eyes but these eyes' is assuredly and proudly declamatory, while 'End in love in the end' seem appropriately lame, at least not agile. An almost lumbering movement comes out of the impending inversion and suspended point of 'A Deep-Sworn Vow':

> Others because you did not keep
> That deep-sworn vow have been friends of mine;
> Yet always when I look death in the face,
> When I clamber to the heights of sleep,
> Or when I grow excited with wine,
> Suddenly I meet your face.

Here the repetition of 'face' is separated by three lines, not a large space when we consider the brevity of the whole. Its repetition comes loudly to the ear as the poem's conspicuously single refusal of rhyme. Her face replaces death's face in a happy replacement, and the ring of genuine feeling owes something to the return to the already used non-rhyming word. No other will do.

The linguistic confinement which so artfully plays at artlessness is seen at its most proficiently cunning in 'Memory':

> One had a lovely face,
> And two or three had charm,
> But charm and face were in vain
> Because the mountain grass
> Cannot but keep the form
> Where the mountain hare has lain.

It repeats and interweaves 'face' and 'charm', as if these things were (unthinkably) interchangeable. It then parallels 'the mountain grass' with the 'mountain hare'. The image of the hare, emblem of elusive fleetness, wildness, and grace is set against the massiveness and sweetness, of the image of mountain grass, and the soft impressionability of grass, modified by the solidity of mountain to make impressed 'form' especially durable. Yeats is good at the poetry of detumescence, and the finality of the ending suggests not only the hare's homecoming, but a heavy pressing down, sexual force moving into sexual peace. But the poem's happiest moment is surely the pun in 'form', which takes repetition to its logical and passionate conclusion. Juxtaposition (like that of the eyes and the faces) becomes union, the hare's bed, lair or 'form' leaves its shape. It happens in one word, but less through a brilliant feat of invention than through the rich benefits conferred by the language. The poet is able to confirm his declaration of union and affinity through a wit large enough and natural enough to ring with sincerity. All he does is to perceive knowledge and gratefully use the semantic insight that the hare's bed was made by its form, so takes form for its name. It is hard to know whether to say that this is the quiet compliment of abdicated art, or an immense hyperbole which involves the natural eloquence of language to praise love, beauty, and faithfulness.

The imagination is content to say 'image' or 'face', simply and without specification. Within these one-breath poems some phrases are especially simple, 'I had a beautiful friend', or 'Suddenly I see your face'. Conversational speech, brevity, and repetition combine to convey intense, honest, strong, or pure feeling. In the later example, 'After Long Silence', addressed (though not explicitly) to Olivia Shakespear, the only repetition in the printed versions is the declamatory crescendo of 'we descant and yet again descant', but there is a prose manuscript draft[1] which shows another instance of repetition like those of the earlier declarations. It is simple and almost matter-of-fact, 'Your hair is white my hair is white'.

Yeats is a clever and passionate poet, but not often a wit. Shakespeare and Donne rely on wit to express love's complications and tensions, and can also withdraw it to achieve stunning simplicity. It is hard to think of great love poetry without some such moments where art appears to give up its artifice to satisfy the experience of inarticulate or humbly worded affections and excitements: 'I wonder by my troth what thou and I/Did till we loved', or 'From you I have been absent in the spring'. The simplicities of Yeats's short poems rely not on wit but on knots of intensification. Such bare and minimal diction and form, contrast strongly with his more proficient elegancies and subtleties. Simplicity is only one eloquent expression of the contemplation of fidelity, though there are local feelings of injury, anger, jealousy, and resentment which flicker as transient but natural expressions across the steady countenance of love. Equally eloquent are the movements of conjunction which make the love poetry seem so actively loving. Words seem to clear a space, or to move close, not so much converting experience into art as behaving appropriately.

In 'The Circus Animals' Desertion' Yeats comes to say 'I must be satisfied with my heart', but the lyrics of simple statement poems show an earlier ability to be so satisfied. Not all the circus animals run away. Crazy Jane, anticipated by Winny Byrne amongst her rags, in *The Tales of Red Hanrahan*, was perfectly at home in the foul rag-and-bone shop where the poet eventually decided to lie down. Yeats shrugged off 'Lion and woman and the Lord Knows what', but he was able to write more directly and particularly. It would not be accurate to say that the poems I have been discussing are non-mythological, since the actual cherishing of the image seems to make a myth, but the poetry is so reflectively aware of that making, as to preserve the sense of individual experience. Maud Gonne's image becomes much more emblematic in the form of lion, woman, rose, child, eagle, bronze head, horse, or hollow cheek wind-drunk. Even in some of the more plainly mythological love poetry the language itself preserves, or creates, the contours of particular feeling. Yeats's brooding contemplation of propinquity and conjunc-

---

[1] Richard Ellmann, *The Identity of Yeats* (London, 1954), Appendix.

tion continued, taking new forms. In 'Against Unworthy Praise' (*The Green Helmet and Other Poems*, 1910) the meetings of words are subtly eloquent:

> O heart, be at peace, because
> Nor knave nor dolt can break
> What's not for their applause,
> Being for a woman's sake.
> Enough if the work has seemed,
> So did she your strength renew,
> A dream that a lion had dreamed
> Till the wilderness cried aloud,
> A secret between you two,
> Between the proud and the proud.
>
> What, still you would have their praise!
> But here's a haughtier text,
> The labyrinth of her days
> That her own strangeness perplexed;
> And how what her dreaming gave
> Earned slander, ingratitude,
> From self-same dolt and knave;
> Aye, and worse wrong than these.
> Yet she, singing upon her road,
> Half lion, half child, is at peace.

In 'the proud and the proud' the epithets lie close to each other, prides joined by love or likeness. The image of the lion will not quite do for the woman, on its own, nor directly for the poet, though perhaps for his inspiration, 'A dream that a lion had dreamed'.

This is a poem which generalises passion, summing up and assessing, remembering and arguing. But even in his poems of particular occasions, we always find the poet's contemplation not only of his passionate experience but also of his image-making, the kind of blend found in 'The Lover Mourns the Loss of Love'. A strange and difficult poem, whose strangeness is not too difficult to be deeply moving, is one of the poems of married love, 'Towards Break of Day' (*Michael Robartes and the Dancer*, 1921). The stimulus of cold dawn gleams from the outer world into the separate sleeps of the lovers, to join them and to separate. The particulars are so startling that they can permit the daring of a

simple statement, 'Nothing that we love over-much/Is ponderable to
our touch'. Its immediate reference is to his childhood memory of the
waterfall on Ben Bulben, narrow, cold, and white like the dawn outside the closed eyes. He cannot return to it as it was, either in dream,
memory, or physical touch. The image of imponderable love attaches
itself to the woman's mysterious and bitter dream of the white leaping
stag, also a reflection of the dawn's light, and more generally still, to
the sense of human closeness and disjunction.

In another poem from the same volume 'An Image from a Past Life',
Maud Gonne's old bed-haunting image returns to be feared, contemplated, shut out, and dismissed. The image comes from the man's
past life but is unseen by him, and sensed by him only through the
woman's terror:

> *He.* Why have you laid your hands upon my eyes?
> What can have suddenly alarmed you
> Whereon 'twere best
> My eyes should never rest?
> What is there but the slowly fading west,
> The river imaging the flashing skies,
> All that to this moment charmed you?
>
> *She.* A sweetheart from another life floats there
> As though she had been forced to linger
> From vague distress
> Or arrogant loveliness,
> Merely to loosen out a tress
> Among the starry eddies of her hair
> Upon the paleness of a finger.

It is her image of desperate and threatened insecurity which has to be
the medium through which the old ghost presses, first ambiguously and
not identified, an 'Image of poignant recollection', then claimed by the
woman as 'An image of my heart that is smitten through'. The poem
proves what its speaker claims, that there is no real threat, that the only
images which can have power are those that would make him 'fonder'.
She covers his eyes, to make sure, and the image is defeated, humiliated,
and put in its place. Yeats explained the image in terms of his mythology, as an Over Shadower, but the power of the poem is immediately
intelligible in other, and simpler human terms. The complicity of the

images is novel, like the experience, showing itself in doubt, denial, and a new allegiance, disturbed but not mastered by the old complicity. The old and the new conjunctions are worked out in the drama of imagery, and the old image is punished.

We return to Maud Gonne's image in ' A Bronze Head' (*Last Poems*, 1936–9) where propinquity is explicitly discussed as bringing 'Imagination to that pitch where it casts out/All that is not itself'. It is also proved in the poem, through the pattern of feeling. The man remembers the woman's young recklessness which drove him wild, though the speech of his wildness is most gentle, 'My child, my child!' The gentleness has already been attributed to the woman (rather startlingly, as has been observed by Marjorie Perloff).[1] The reason for the attribution is plain. If she is wild, as is demonstrated, so must he be, though this is assumed without being shown. There are things that love poems, like lovers, have to take for granted. The taking for granted is most moving in this poem of remembered youth and power.

The trajectory of feeling in Yeats is sometimes wild, especially when describing wildness. Amongst those poems which seem both meditative and dramatic, he responds to particular occasions but refuses to let them serve as simple objective correlatives for feeling, since Yeats knew something not pointed out by Eliot, that occasions do not always oblige in that way. In 'A Memory of Youth' (*Responsibilities*, 1914) there is an arbitrary shift from the usual miserable lover's acknowledgment that love hasn't a future to a radiant surprised exhilaration. Its origin is left opaque and mysterious, since we are told that, 'the cry/Of a most ridiculous little bird/Tore from the clouds his marvellous moon'. The image stands poised on the border of actuality and metaphor, refusing to allow us to settle for either, indifferent to causality. The balance of feeling tilts startlingly.

In the same volume is the poem 'The Cold Heaven' in which Yeats uncomfortably enlarges the scope of amorous feeling. He draws on amorous tension and remorse to make the purgatorial nightmare physically present, assaulting the nerves. At the same time the conjunctions and complicities of love are deepened by the supernatural into vision. Religion and love play hysterically but profoundly into each other's hands:

[1] Marjorie G. Perloff, ' "Heart Mysteries": The Later Love Lyrics of W. B. Yeats', *Contemporary Literature*, x, 1969, pp. 266–83.

And I took all the blame out of all sense and reason,
Until I cried and trembled and rocked to and fro,
Riddled with light.

In 'Her Vision in the Wood' (*The Winding Stair and Other Poems,* 1933) Yeats again brings off this enlargement of *odi et amo.* The poem begins with a sexual longing and a self-desecration. The vision in the wood is invoked by this desperate auto-erotic invocation:

Dry timber under that rich foliage,
At wine-dark midnight in the sacred wood,
Too old for a man's love I stood in rage
Imagining men. Imagining that I could
A greater with a lesser pang assuage
Or but to find if withered vein ran blood,
I tore my body that its wine might cover
Whatever could recall the lip of lover.

The fearful lovers in 'A Memory of Youth' and 'A Cold Heaven' invoke experience, good or bad, which is more than they bargained for, and the woman's vision is appallingly appropriate. Its blood is invoked by her blood, and its pang and wound by her pang and wound. Her recall of love is apparently reversed in the deathly procession. There is a weird complicity between her *fiat*, made by memory, imagination and blood, and the art of the pall-bearers, who sing of the beast and the wound. She sings with them, but her 'malediction' seems to attach itself to the singers in her attack on this youth and stateliness, 'Why should they think that they are for ever young?' The aesthetic image is abhorrent. The malediction seems so far removed from the 'beast that gave the fatal wound', that it is also ready to be directed at the 'blood-bedabbled breast', so that the actual recognition of her 'heart's victim and its torturer' is curiously preceded by the passion. This reversal of cause and effect strengthens the feeling that the vision has been invoked by the extremity of desire, the unassuaged longing forcing and finding only death, as blood calls to blood, and her limbs, and his breast are matched in injury. Complicity and conjunction are terrifying. And the last stanza ensures a greater shock, as she recognises that no fabulous symbol is there, and as we recognise with her the fabulous symbol, the wounded Adonis. To recognise him is to recognise her, as his torturer and his victim, as Venus humanised or a Venus-like

woman.[1] To recognise her is to understand the violence of that unassuaged desire and desecration, literally aphrodisiac. Lusts, pangs and
fiat are now elucidated. To say that it is a myth particularised is to dam-
pen its fires. It is a myth related with a frightening innocence and
knowingness to elucidate and to possess us in active ritual.

Yeats's erotic range includes the wicked, ironic joke of 'Consolation'
(*The Winding Stair and Other Poems*, 1933) whose words mime the
act of love in a kind of sly flaunting, and the bizarre use of the innocents
in 'News for the Delphic Oracle' (*Last Poems*, 1936–9), whose wounds
open with a sexual bite in that salt wave. There is the unperturbed,
curious eye of the chambermaid clearly seeing the detumescent 'worm'
in 'The Three Bushes' (*Last Poems*, 1936–9), and its nice oblique use of
sexually suggestive sounds:

> That I may hear if we should kiss
> A contrapuntal serpent hiss,
> You, should hand explore a thigh,
> All the labouring heavens sigh.

Sensuality in Yeats is always dramatised, attached to the eyes and
limbs of some defined person, an outraged newsgiver, the detached and
never passionately involved maid, dirty old men and women loving
to boast and shock, though never merely to boast and shock. Indeed,
Yeats said that when Jane seemed to be getting too promiscuous and
disgusting, he had to kill her off. An impressive testimony to the power
of images. In 'A Last Confession' (*The Winding Stair and Other Poems*,
1933), the erotic detail of undressing, clinging and embracing defines
conjunction which goes beyond the sexuality, both in the negative,
purely physical act, and in the ideal instance:

> What lively lad most pleasured me
> Of all that with me lay?
> I answer that I gave my soul

---

[1] She is also Grania, as her Adonis is Dermid. Yeats may even be echoing or
remembering Samuel Ferguson's poem 'The Death of Dermid', *Lays of the
Western Gael*, 1865, some of whose details speak for themselves:
> Close-pack'd thy fingers then, thong-drawn and squeezed,
> The blood-drops oozing under every nail,
> When, like a shadow, through the sleeping priests
> Came I, and loos'd thee . . .

And loved in misery,
But had great pleasure with a lad
That I loved bodily.

Flinging from his arms I laughed
To think his passion such
He fancied that I gave a soul
Did but our bodies touch,
And laughed upon his breast to think
Beast gave beast as much.

I gave what other women gave
That stepped out of their clothes,
But when this soul, its body off,
Naked to naked goes,
He it has found shall find therein
What none other knows,

And give his own and take his own
And rule in his own right;
And though it loved in misery
Close and cling so tight,
There's not a bird of day that dare
Extinguish that delight.

In 'Crazy Jane on the Day of Judgment' it is her sourness and nakedness that insists on soul as well as body, the extreme physicality that claims more than physicality for love. In 'Crazy Jane and Jack the Journeyman' words are repeated and varied to brood over the two kinds of love: the word 'skein' fits the casual winding and unwinding of sex, in its thoroughly imagined image, and freshly fits the aftermath of promiscuous embracing, something meaningless to be left on the ground, defleshed like a mere skin. In the final stanza the skein is exalted, and its binding power is used to invoke a hank of cords that joins 'ghost with ghost'. The vision of the illuminated house is seen by Jane whose body is 'like a road/That men pass over', her words to the Bishop are an explanation of her role as spokeswoman for flesh and spirit, her truth 'Learned in bodily lowliness/And in the heart's pride'.

The appreciation of wholeness depends on the knowledge of desecration:

> But Love has pitched his mansion in
> The place of excrement;
> For nothing can be sole or whole
> That has not been rent.

Her insight, 'Love is like the lion's tooth', does more than awaken an old image, as its refrain endorses or is endorsed by the demonstrations of the dancers who 'had all that had their hate', and are dancing and thus coupled, animated, ordered, even in wildness.

Yeats does not, like Donne, put aside amorous verse. Crazy Jane lies down in the poet's rag-and-bone shop of the heart. Through her, Yeats, like Donne and others, uses amorous language for religious experience, but not metaphorically, insisting on sexuality itself as a means of transcendent knowledge. Religion can only offer metaphors for love. Jane pleads experience, but after all this is hard to prove, especially for a fiction, and perhaps we can only say that her energy, and extremity of feeling imply the necessary courage and knowledge for faith and discrimination in love. Her extremities of passion can at least rebuke the Church, which expects her to have one foot in the grave, whereas she is making love on its very edge.

A rather more dignified character, who also makes love on the grass, but not for lack of soft beds, is Sheba. She also brings courage and abandon, to produce a visionary celebration. Like Jane, though more gently, she also brings humour. So too does Solomon, touting union, constancy, and joy so vigorously as to startle if not quite transcend ordinary experience. Yeats praised *Lady Chatterley's Lover* for its 'forlorn poetry ... ancient, humble and terrible',[1] and might have used obscenity well in his poetry, which sometimes seems to want to be obscene. But there is no need to patronise or lament Yeats's dignified language. The dignity of 'love has pitched his mansion in/The place of excrement', does not impair its force, and he is able to be not only violent but even amusing about uninhibited sexuality and perversion because of the grand language used to describe them. He came to admire Lawrence, but could certainly do without him. When Lawrence prepared to die, erotic experience seemed to fall away, and 'The

---

[1] Letter to Olivia Shakespear, 22 May 1933, *Letters of W. B. Yeats*, ed. Allan Wade (London, 1954).

Ship of Death' is a preparation for the spirit's journey without the
sexual body, but Yeats's poetry of old age was full of urges and crav-
ings. The sequence, 'A Man Young and Old' (*The Tower*, 1928) contains some of the quietest erotic poetry Yeats wrote. But its bitterness
is an important tone in his love poetry. It uses the principle of conjunction ironically, to mark the losses of memory and the memory of
losses, the more effectively for catching at romantic images such as
moon and mermaid. Images, like the moon, appear innocently, but
their innocence and glamour is dismissed violently, though in their
own terms, 'every hand is lunatic/That travels on the moon'. Propinquity works here with cruel echoes, sounding echoes across the individual poems in the sequence. A woman's heart of stone becomes his
'bit of stone', the stone becomes the imaginary child which mad,
barren Madge wraps up and nurses, then appears again when Peter
perches on it to boast, as Yeats once did, that he was King of the Pea-
cocks. The shriek is a key image inside and outside this sequence. It is
the shriek he would like to utter in the heart's agony which in dumb
dignity he restrains, the amorous shriek 'the first of all the tribe' refrains from sounding in sexual climax, then Peter's boastful peacock-
shriek, and finally his own recollection 'that her shriek was love/And
that he shrieks from pride'. The sequence ends with a joining of the
images, in a longing to 'mount and sail up there/Amid the cloudy
wrack', casually substituting Paris for Peter in a brilliant sleight-of-hand
like some of the old mythologising, and ending:

> Were I but there and none to hear
> I'd have a peacock cry,
> For that is natural to a man
> That lives in memory,
> Being all alone I'd nurse a stone
> And sing it lullaby.

This rough eloquence says harshly that the shared images show the
shared life, bed of straw or down, what matter? This is reduction, and
attrition. But of course it is not a last word, only one of many tones.

Erich Heller's essay on Yeats and Nietzsche[1] puts in its place the
inclination to praise 'Michael Robartes and the Dancer' (*Michael
Robartes and the Dancer*, 1921) for its charm, but perhaps charm may be
ascribed to 'The Gift of Harun Al-Rashid' (*The Tower*, 1928) and

---

[1] Erich Heller, 'Yeats and Nietzsche', *Encounter*, xxxiii, 1969, pp. 64–72.

'Solomon and the Witch' (*Michael Robartes and the Dancer*, 1921). In these poems the puzzle about image and person takes a different form. 'Solomon and the Witch' is Yeats's comic version of Donne's witty 'The Extasie' and can similarly confound critics who find it hard to take the combination of mysticism, eroticism, and humour. The joke lies not in the location of vision and bed, in a marriage—an excellent place for it—but in the presentation of the serious argument in terms of sexual gusto. The inarticulate chatter of the animals, which Solomon can understand, may not stand precisely for orgasmic shrieking, but sounds its loud, strident, demented, and irrational row in a suggestive analogy. Sheba cries out 'in a strange tongue/Not his, not mine', and the cry is immediately put beside the clamour of the animals, presumably during, and probably at the climax of, the act of love:

> Who understood
> Whatever has been said, sighed, sung,
> Howled, miau-d, barked, brayed, belled, yelled, cried, crowed...

This is a likely bridebed, the images found being remarkably close to those expected, contrary to general experience, 'Chance being at one with Choice at last'. The moon in the poem is both wild and blessed, and becomes even wilder on the second night. Yeats is grave, but amused as well, as he feels able to plead at one and the same time for another try at ending the world, redeeming the Fall, and making love endlessly. Solomon, like Yeats, is doubtful but affectionately good-tempered about the strength of the image. Sheba speaks and Solomon answers:

> 'Yet the world stays.'
> > 'If that be so,
> Your cockerel found us in the wrong
> Although he thought it worth a crow.
> Maybe an image is too strong
> Or maybe is not strong enough.'

But Sheba proves Yeats's insistence that the best thoughts are thought in a marrow-bone. Her persuasion is sly, erotic, not quite brazen, and funny, as she pursues the argument, and seizes on the abstract excuse to return with the philosopher to bed and bedrock. Yeats's contemplations and passions shift acts and images prolifically and resiliently:

> 'O Solomon, let us try again.'

6

The Reticence of W. H. Auden

I

Auden is always talking about the feeling behind poems and in poems, whether he is classifying poetic kinds, or defining sources of poetic power, or recoiling—with some sympathy—from the unrestrained out-pourings of Lawrence, or responding in warm fellow-feeling to the austerity of Frost. His interest in the relation between the feeling behind the poem and the feeling in the poem is there in the disingenuous banter of 'The Truest Poetry is the Most Feigning' (*The Shield of Achilles*) and in the careful unpeeling of the reasons why a certain poem cannot be written in 'Dichtung Und Wahrheit' (*Homage to Clio*). But even his more sympathetic critics talk about him as a poet writing just from the head. G. S. Fraser, for instance, would either like to like Auden better than he does or else likes him more than he thinks he should, and the three essays in *Vision and Rhetoric* (London, 1959) sound a 'Vorrei e non vorrei' of goodwill and disapproval. Actually, if everything Fraser says about Auden were true, then he ought to be really ferocious: Auden lacks 'personal immediacy' and 'has never been interested either in his own experience, or the experience of other people, for its own sake; he has been interested in it as an instance of a general case, of the sort of thing that happens'. It is not surprising that Fraser does not think that Auden is 'fundamentally a religious poet', finds no evidence in the volume *For the Time Being* of 'any profound *personal* spiritual experience' and feels sure that the religious thinking is not new but to be found in 'Sir, no man's enemy'.

My contention is that Auden *is* interested in personal experience and that he writes the kind of poetry which engages us, in every sense of the word, by the recognisable voice of personal feeling. It is sad to find feeling left out of Monroe Spears's list of Auden's poetic attractions 'entertainment, instruction, intellectual excitement, and a prodigal variety of aesthetic pleasures'. I suppose feeling might be tucked away among those prodigal pleasures, though it certainly gets scant attention in the scholarly exegesis of *The Poetry of W. H. Auden* (New York,

1963). Spears cannot be entirely forgiven for this neglect on the grounds that his concern is purely conceptual. His observations on Auden's technique are fascinatingly and consistently reminiscent of the sort of thing Auden himself says we tend to say about emotionless aesthetic Ariel-poems (like Peele's beautiful 'Bathsabe's Song'): 'If one tries to explain why one likes the song, or any poem of this kind, one finds oneself talking about language, the handling of the rhythm, the pattern of vowels and consonants, the placing of caesuras, epanorthosis, etc.' I think this list should bring a faint blush to Professor Spears's cheek. Of course he knows that Auden is not an Ariel-poet, because Ariel-poets are not interested in serious matters, but he does not share Auden's proper assumption that an interest in serious matters ought to involve the heart as well as the head. Or if he does, it does not show.

It might have shown to advantage, for instance, when Spears calls 'The Prophets' a religious poem in which Auden is entertaining Christianity rather than fully believing in it, but says the 'Epilogue' (to *New Year Letter*) seems fully committed. Like Fraser, Spears talks about religious poetry without looking closely at questions of feeling and he seems to be excessively interested in finding 'evidence' for belief *in* the poetry.

More important and less misleading than this talk about entertaining beliefs is the observation I have already quoted that Speech, as an artistic language, has the 'serious defect' of lacking the Indicative Mood: 'all its statements are in the subjunctive and only possibly true until verified (which is not always possible) by non-verbal evidence' ('Dichtung Und Wahrheit'). The difference between 'The Prophets' and the 'Epilogue' seems to me to lie in the decorous presence in the one and decorous absence in the other of transitive feeling and its personal voice. I would call 'The Prophets' a poem which had religious feeling (never mind about 'evidence' for profound spiritual experiences) and the 'Epilogue' a poem which discussed religion and the context for belief without needing to express feeling about God in a transitive form. The difference between 'The Prophets' and 'Sir, no man's enemy' seems to me to lie in the decorous feeling in the first and the indecorous lack of feeling in the second. 'Sir, no man's enemy' is cast coldly and arbitrarily in the form of prayer (or strikes us as cold and arbitrary) because it shows none of the feeling prayer ought to have for the God it prays to, no trust or affection or doubt or fear or anguish, and none of the feeling of wanting and sorely needing the things being prayed for. Compare it with Herbert or Donne or with the Hopkins prayer-sonnet, 'Thou art indeed just, Lord, if I contend/With thee; but, sir, so what I plead is just', to which it may perhaps owe the idea of God not being an enemy as well as the feudal-religious Sir.

But it is best compared with a poem by Auden. 'The Prophets' has the authentic-sounding voice of love, and even shows Auden using the 'natural style' he snipes at as unnatural in 'The Truest Poetry'. It was written, by the way, in 1939 and so had the advantage of getting into *Another Time*, whereas Auden's other religious poems of the Forties ('Kairos and Logos', 'In Sickness and Health' and others) may have been neglected because they never appeared in a small separate volume but got lost in the random arrangement and reprinted poems of *Collected Shorter Poems*.[1] 'The Prophets' begins with a compressed and oblique account of those prophetic relationships of love and reverence which prepared the poet for belief, and moves into a climax of joyful and trusting recognition. God is never actually named and some readers on the way to understanding the poem are—just about—able to read it as a poem about human love:

> For now I have the answer from the face
> That never will go back into a book
> But asks for all my life, and is the Place
> Where all I touch is moved to an embrace,
> And there is no such thing as a vain look.

The Eureka-feeling at the end has a finality and faith and identification that some poets include in the range of human love, but not Auden. The point I want to emphasise is that the poem depends on expressing this feeling of relationship. The possibility that Auden never actually experienced this feeling outside the poem—he may have been trying out a fantasy about discovering God, or imitating someone else's experience or transferring the romantic 'You at last' feeling to a religious context which it could realistically inhabit, or recording a dream (Eureka-feelings can be most impressive in dreams)—seems beside the point.

[1] All references are to the 1950 edition of *Collected Shorter Poems*.

II

'The Prophets' is rare in its direct and simple unbaring of feeling. At the
end of 'The Truest Poetry' Auden says '. . . love, or truth in any serious
sense,/Like orthodoxy, is a reticence'. In the Prologue to *The Dyer's Hand*
he says '"Orthodoxy"', said a real Alice of a bishop, '"is reticence"'.
(I do not know the reference.) 'The Prophets' is a discreet and quiet
poem, but many of Auden's expressions of relationship are much more
reticent. The reticence takes many forms, not all of them quiet. Strident
imperatives, casual sloppiness of word and phrase, exaggeratedly rigid
doggerel, extravagant hyperbole, 'clinical' coldness, many kinds of
anti-climax, all can be forms for his reticence. The anti-rhetoric of such
devices often gives a serious appearance of urgency or passion or desperation or mission which has no time to concern itself overmuch with
art. Prospero can deliberately try to do without Ariel. But Auden
seldom if ever slips into purely imitative maladroit form: he will give
the appearance of mechanical regularity or contemptuous speed or
facile casualness or cheap wit, but when one comes to analyse (best of
all, especially in the case of verse-form, to imitate) these racy reticences
it soon becomes apparent that much art has gone into their artlessness.
A good example is 'Heavy Date', a 'light' love poem which sounds
as if it was dashed off spontaneously like the random thinking which is
its ostensible subject but which is metrically most carefully regularised,
like its train of thought which takes us to a skilfully contrived conclusion.

It would of course be quite wrong to suggest that all Auden's styles
are styles for reticence. Almost every volume from 1930 onwards has
one poem or more written in a grand or, let us say, 'ceremonious' style,
using dignified vocabulary, formal syntax, and solemn intricate har-
monies. There are the sober meditations of '1929', the sonorous
sestinas of 'Kairos and Logos' and the very disturbing 'Memorial for
the City' with its moving and dignified conclusion in plain speech: 'I
was the missing entry in Don Giovanni's list; for which he could never
account'. Auden has used 'the wry, the sotto-voce,/Ironic and mono-
chrome' throughout his writing, but never as an exclusive style. His
reticence often takes an oblique or teasing form for feeling, but there
are many poems, like these, which use a simply appropriate form, a
conventional decorum.

III

But there is one style of reticence which runs through all his work, beginning in the 1928 volume. This whole volume (*pace* Monroe Spears, who says that its 'most obvious characteristic is the detached, clinical, objective attitude, with modern and scientific imagery') has the appearance of being deeply rooted—perhaps too deeply rooted—in personal experience. (The one obvious exception is a poem in the manner of Hardy, No. XII, 'The four sat on in the bare room'.) Some of the most obscure poems, such as No. 1, which appears to be a seven-part poem about a love-affair, traced through moments of crisis, only some of which seem to rise into moving definition, are probably obscure because half-embedded in private experience, meaningful to a particular reader who could read between the lines, localise the images, and recognise the feeling. But this is just a guess, made not in the interests of speculation but because Auden's successful reticence seems to be the minimal public emergence of this kind of private experience. Auden has often been accused of vagueness, but it might be more appropriate to call it over-specification. Nothing is so vague in its effect as the highly particularised reference which we do not happen to understand, and it is this, rather than emotional swimminess, which is characteristic of Auden's very early verse. But when he does achieve the minimal lucidity there is a very compelling effect of being let in on a real feeling which we can feel without knowing its history and causality. This is, I suggest, the effect of Poem XI, probably the most familiar of the 1928 Poems because reprinted in *Collected Shorter Poems* as 'The Love Letter' and in the Penguin Selection as 'The Letter'. This is the unrevised version:

> From the very first coming down
> Into a new valley with a frown
> Because of the sun and a lost way
> You certainly remain. Today
> I, crouching behind a sheep-pen, heard
> Travel across a sudden bird,
> Cry out against the storm, and found
> The year's arc a completed round
> And love's worn circuit rebegun
> Endless with no dissenting turn.

Shall see, shall pass, as we have seen
The swallow on the tiles, Spring's green
Preliminary shiver, passed
A solitary truck, the last
Of shunting in the Autumn; but now,
To interrupt the homely brow,
Thought warmed to evening through and through,
Your letter comes, speaking as you
Speaking of much but not to come.
Nor speech is close, nor fingers numb
If love not seldom has received
An unjust answer, was deceived;
I, decent with the seasons, move
Different or with a different love,
Nor question overmuch the nod,
The stone smile of this country god,
That never was more reticent,
Always afraid to say more than it meant,

It seems to be a poem about two letters, the one received and the reply, which is the poem itself. At least the poem is transitive, addressed to You. It begins with a brief and understated comment on the beginning and the duration of the love:' You certainly remain' expresses its feeling very quietly. There are two times in the poem: the ignorant past when he was alone in the storm, remembering and still believing in a future: 'love's worn circuit rebegun/Endless with no dissenting turn', and the time after he got the letter, which casts its shadow on the reported past so that 'frown', 'lost way', 'worn circuit', and 'shiver' all belong to both times and can be read as both innocently appropriate to the past and ominously appropriate to the future. The exposure, storm, crying out of the bird, and the solitude are all sources of compression, and say in a laconic enactment what the situation was and is. The letter which breaks the news is also described laconically, 'Speaking of much but not to come'. The feeling of love, hope, and the loss of hope are not enlarged on. Feeling is not described at all, but implied by the reticent form and language, which decorously convey the pressure of the feeling which is controlled in decent silence. The knotted negatives of 'Nor speech is close', the impersonal form of 'If love not seldom has received', the compression of the movement to 'was deceived', the ellipsis and shift of tense which seems to blur out this particular instance, all contribute to the reticence. The double time and its emotional duplicity, the clipped style, and the refusal to express direct feeling, all quietly weigh feeling and evaluate as they define. Thus the poem is not merely one which sets up a tension between austere form and strong unexpressed feeling, but is, or becomes, a poem about reticence. 'I, decent with the seasons' uses decency in the sense of propriety, passing on properly as the seasons pass on (they are all stated or implied in the poem). It also suggests the decency of taking things quietly, without fuss, with a stiff upper lip. And the final significant appearance of the landscape is to create a climactic image of reticence: the reticence which withholds the explanation one may desperately ask of gods and nature, the reticence which is at least not deceitful—someone may have said more than they meant in the submerged past of this love—and the reticence which is that of the poem itself, which is perhaps not about breaking your heart in decent silence but about not breaking it. The loss is endurable, and an extravagant grief would be out of place and perhaps dishonest. The austerity and compression of the poem is a perfect form for the austerity and restraint which it discusses, and the form is dynamic, taking us on in time, taking us through a moving process of feeling. We may at one stage think that the reticence means stoicism, but at the end it merely means honesty. The lack of history and character and causality throws the full weight upon the feeling, which is neither cold nor vague, though it is just possible to see that its austerity might be misread as detachment without passion and that its vagueness about the unnecessary elements might be found obscure by readers who wanted fuller and more obviously exciting 'treatment'.

IV

This minimal anecdote which suppresses almost everything but feeling, which has a reticence of concentrated passion, and which asserts the privacy of the relationship as an essential part of love for individuals and God, seems to me to be Auden's most original and characteristic achievement as a love poet. It is of course not his only manner in love-poetry and is clearly less popular than the fuller anecdote in 'Lay your sleeping head, my love', much anthologised and in my view much less interesting. It dramatises fairly fully a situation and a locale (time, place, position), has characters with some characteristics, and gives us a compressed but fairly elaborate reflection on love in general, its likeness and unlikeness to religious ecstasy, its powers and limitations, its social vulnerability. It attempts to place the future of the relationship and the beloved both realistically and affectionately. It has the have-your-cake-and-eat-it sophistication of Byron (and is indeed rather like the description of Juan asleep in Haidée's arms, 'There lies the thing we love with all its errors'), but its interest seems to me to be chiefly the interest of a story rather than a dynamic evaluation or definition of feeling of the kind to be found in 'The Letter'. The two first published volumes, *Poems* (1930) and *Look, Stranger!*, have their share of austere and reticent love poems. In 'Upon this line between adventure' and 'To lie on the back, the knees flexed' compression and suppression are used for more erotic subjects, where the concentration of feeling and the privacy have their special effects of tension and intimacy.

Many of these poems of the thirties have a personal subject which is often overlooked in their political context, just as the feeling in some of the religious poetry is unnoticed—at least by the critics—perhaps because of the sheer conceptual difficulty and interest. At times, of course, the personal emotion is subordinated to the political subject, as in '1929'. At times the two are held in dramatic tension, as in 'A Summer Night, 1933', where the personal relationship stands as representative of a community, stands for the sheltered, expensive, cultivated, pleasurable, furtive, insecure, loving privileges of a certain class, which must go but which can perhaps bequeath at least the powers of love.

One of my reasons for drawing attention to Auden's love poetry is that it indicates the importance of the personal voice elsewhere, in the religious and political verse, which both depend on the transitive expression of love as Eros and Agape mutate. But the personal voice addressed to the special reader can come in almost gratuitously, to give not an appropriate feeling to a poem about God or society but an unexpected influx of personal feeling in a fairly impersonal poem. In *Nones*, for instance, we find several instances of the way personal feeling can flood a poem with immediacy and warmth and can give the impression that it is steadily available. In 'In Praise of Limestone' there is a point towards the end—at the beginning of the last stanza—when into a meditative line is suddenly inserted 'My Dear', though with as yet no change in the tone or feeling. It is a tiny pre-echo, a faint heralding of the most moving turn to address a particular person at the very end of the poem:

> ... Dear, I know nothing of
> Either, but when I try to imagine a faultless love
> Or the life to come, what I hear is the murmur
> Of underground streams, what I see is a limestone landscape.

It comes as the kind of surprise which, once taken in, seems natural and inevitable. The poem has no transitive appearance until the first 'my dear', and even then it is only preparatory. This is a reticence, too, transforming the poem's form and giving the impression of a love which is in the background not because removed from other considerations but because it can always move easily into the forefront of any subject, being the most important feeling, the most important person. The poem alludes with the ease of confident (but not over-confident) love to this particular reader, but its warmth extends also to the 'life to come' and the limestone landscape. There is a beautiful decorum in the way the subject of love brings in the loving tone, especially since the question of imagining faultless love has come up, and the human lover might require to be confronted and not excluded. But the personal feeling also acts as a medium for the feeling for God and nature. Auden's withholding of the personal tone until the end permits him to make a climax beyond the capacity of the earlier intransitive meditation.

This is a kind of reticence which permits strong feeling to break through briefly. Sometimes the break is comically affectionate, as in 'Compline':

> ... *libera*
> *Me, libera C* (dear C).

But the reticence of feeling does not emerge only in parenthesis or understatement. It can inhabit a whole poem, as it did in the 1928 volume. Auden has, however, in the later volumes a predilection for a kind of double-take poem, where the subject and tones of love are very late in declaring themselves and where the capacity for climax of 'In Praise of Limestone' is shown in a rather different context, not added on to an already meaningful poetic assertion but coming in order to complete a passage whose meaning is not grasped until the emotion finally gives the key. In 'Serenade' (*Nones*) we have a love poem which does not declare itself until the last four lines, after two stanzas and a half which accumulate a series of images—cataracts, diplomats, children and tigers—of public declaration, axe-grinding, relationship. The point of the poem is that such needs are the explanation for love:

> So, my embodied love
> Which, like most feeling, is
> Half humbug, and half true,
> Asks neighbourhood of you.

The withholding of subject has once more the effect of release and relief: the reticence is there in the rather elaborate talk leading up to the main point and in the revelation of that point. This kind of structure of specious and real subject allows Auden to achieve a truly reticent climax: a quiet observation or understatement falls like a feather but turns the scale. This is creating a special context in which a reticent statement of emotion can sound very loud. In 'Secrets' (*Nones*) we have the same structure used in a religious poem. Again we move slowly step by step through a series of images and instances which accrete a general statement about human curiosity, which in turn is related to the need for human love. But the climax is temporary—it never is a climax of feeling, anyway, merely the impression that we have got to the point— and we move on further until human need is distinguished from God, 'From whom no secrets are hid'.

A most moving reticence is found in 'Their Lonely Betters', a poem in some ways very close to the subject and feeling of 'The Letter' though technically and linguistically very different. This is, like 'Serenade' and 'Secrets', a poem written in a loose and conversational style: its reticence comes chiefly from the structure. The poet first establishes a series of contrasts between animals and humans which looks as if it is going to be another version of some of the animal-human contrasts in the earlier poetry. They were there, however, to define qualities in human beings, necessary conceits by which an argument was conducted. Here the ostensible subject is unimportant and bears an arbitrary relation to the feeling which reveals itself at the end. We end, this time, not with a personal and transitive feeling but with a generalisation about love and need:

> Let them leave language to their lonely betters
> Who count some days and long for certain letters;
> We, too, make noises when we laugh or weep.
> Words are for those with promises to keep.

What looks like impersonal general statement is plainly weighted with personal feeling. Even the vagueness is pointed: 'some days and certain letters'. The austerity is weighted with the feelings of privacy, dignity and control. The end reflects back on the beginning: so this is why he was at a loose end, listening to vegetables and birds and so on. Auden's reticence finds many different forms and some of them seem to show that it is dangerous to assume that a generalisation—in poetry as in life—does not refer to an individual instance. And of course—in poetry as in life—there are many good reasons for reticence.

7

W. H. Auden, Thirties to Sixties: a Face and a Map

An emblem for Auden would be an ambiguous profile looking from one side like a face and from the other like a map. His poems show a fondness for real faces and maps, but the purpose of the emblem would be to express his central and constant fusion of a private and a public world. The facelike map and the maplike face seem to be formed in the imaginative effort to look at private and public worlds at the same time, overlapping, blurred, mutually determining, or interlocked, their distinctiveness often diffused, dissolved, and dissipated.

The mutations of Auden's Eros have been sufficiently discussed, and I should like to take for granted both those special influences that impelled him, like other poets of England in the thirties, into the conscientious association of inner and outer experience, and those later forces that shifted him from a psycho-political to a psycho-religious concept of Love. Though the impulse that relates love to Love in the thirties is shaped by Fascism and Communism, it is also a local and collectivised form of that artistic and moral conscience that more recently made a less rational poet, Sylvia Plath, insist that poetry should relate our private pains and madness to things like Dachau and Hiroshima. In the political and the not-quite-political poetry of the thirties, a relation is made not only between the private and social pain and madness, but also between the private and social feelings of joy, desire, love, indulgence, and indeed all or any aspects of relationship. One of the most original features of Auden's early poetry of love and politics is its exploration of the details of passion and relationship, in which the lineaments of the face are constantly transferred to the map, the contours of the map to the face. We can only speculate about the sources of such an impulse to fusion: they lie in the contemporary political conscience, the compelling and terrible facts, and the Freudian interest in personal and social psychoanalysis. They seem to lie as much in political doubt and uncertainty—perhaps more—as in political conviction, and I disagree very strongly with John Bayley's view that Auden's early political poetry is arrogant, though he happens to be right about his one instance, 'Get there if you can' (*The Romantic Survival*, London, 1957). The association of the inner and outer lives works to elucidate, to complicate, and at times to set up a resistance to what Wallace Stevens calls the increased pressures of reality.

Bernard Spencer, an easier poet than Auden, but often showing the same social pressure on the personal life, has a poem called 'Waiting'. While someone he loves is being operated on, he feels the relation of his fear, imagined pain, and helplessness to the world's crisis, and moves through questioning to conclude that the larger pain has to be tackled by the patient, who is both knowing and capable of action: 'from our crisis leads no white stair to a shut/Door and the deftness of another's hands'. There is no sense that one experience is subordinated or turned into illustration. By rendering one intensity, another is brought out. Two experiences are laid against the other and while the poem's stress is finally placed on the public world, the act of enlargement includes both situations in a sensitive unity.

Auden's poetry often moves to an enlargement and expansion of the private passions, but he can equally often move from the public into the private world. He very rarely produces the simple comparison of the Spencer poem, but tends to work through tension, confusion, and turmoil. His poems are about the moral and psychic complexity of waiting both for an operation and a war, about the actual intensity and obscure sufferings of the two-hearted experience. In Poem XVI of his first formally published volume, *Poems* ('It was Easter as I walked in the public gardens'), there is oscillation from the private life to the public, in a return and recoil that makes both centres of feeling substantial, even though we end in the outer world. In Poem XXI of *Look, Stranger!* ('Easily, my dear, easily you move, easily your head') the imaged growth of Nazism is a matrix of metaphor for a passionate moral address to a person, but the personal passions depend on the strength of the political documentation. In Poem XV in *Look, Stranger!* ('The chimneys are smoking') there is a more obscure and ambivalent conflation of private and political allusiveness. In all these poems, even where there is a sense of final direction and focus, even where one experience is momentarily subordinated to the other, as ground, cause, effect, or symbol, there is a substantial double concern. There is also the sense that the poem, without losing passion, knows what it is up to, that the metaphorical manipulation is superimposed on the real primary experience.

II

Poem XVI from *Poems* is called '1929' in *Collected Shorter Poems*. Its relation to many of Auden's other shorter poems of the thirties is rather like that of 'Tintern Abbey' to much early Wordsworth. Indeed, like 'Tintern Abbey', Auden's poem is highly compressed, fragmented, and brilliantly cut in a wide-ranging elucidation of thinking and feeling. It sets up precise and lucid sensuous particulars, arranged scenically and plucked with an air of fine casualness from the surface of a time (1929) and a place (Germany). It moves in and out of these sensuous images to a series of dynamic and clipped generalisations about the poet's situation, human growth, and an environment of police oppression, misery, war, and revolution. Like 'Tintern Abbey', again, it is good at analysing those very powers of sensation, feeling, and thought that it directly displays, though in his handling of ideas, and his elasticity, immediacy, and polished artifice, Auden is much more like Coleridge, the Coleridge of the conversation poems.[1]

His '1929' begins with the sensuous particulars of a walk in the public gardens in spring. It starts the seasonal rhythm which forms and informs the poem, both as a constant source of fresh particulars and as a structural symbol for the changes of history and personal growth. It also starts off the swing from the inner to the outer world, in a sudden compassionate, and shocking encounter:

> It was Easter as I walked in the public gardens,
> Hearing the frogs exhaling from the pond,
> Watching traffic of magnificent cloud
> Moving without anxiety on open sky—
> Season when lovers and writers find
> An altering speech for altering things,
> An emphasis on new names, on the arm
> A fresh hand with fresh power.

---

[1] Richard Hoggart, in his Introduction to *W. H. Auden: A Selection* (London, 1961), is illuminating on the conversational quality of the verse, but the poem he instances, 'Dover', though fine in its way, is conversational in language rather than structure.

> But thinking so I came at once
> Where solitary man sat weeping on a bench,
> Hanging his head down, with his mouth distorted
> Helpless and ugly as an embryo chicken.

We begin with the personal life, its creativity and sexuality gently and firmly stressed and expressed through time, place, and weather. We come abruptly up against age, impotence, isolation, hopelessness, ugliness. Spring in the public gardens is fine for the young, the lovers, the confident, but old age hangs its head on these benches too. The 'new names', 'fresh hand' and 'fresh power' stand confidently in their wit and suggestiveness both for art and love. The walk and the upward gaze at those unanxious clouds make a strong suggestion of ease and expectancy, but the poet has to come down from the clouds to see humanity hang its weak ugly head in a parody of Easter fertility. The embryo is both a piteous travesty of an Easter chick and a visually incisive caricature of scrawny, floppy age. All the first images and impressions are laid low, and all the properties of the encounter are physically and symbolically complete and precise. The abstraction is attained in an act of feeling: this is pride and joy and personal preoccupation startled, rebuked, made to look and pity. Abstraction is needed, in order to generalise the humanity outside the poet, publicly and anonymously and commonly there, crying for love, hard to love, necessary to love. Abstraction is needed also in order to take us right outside the subjective beginning, outside the inner life in a large and extroverted motion. It is imaginatively impressive detail like this which makes one impatient of those commonplaces about Auden's abstractions which constantly trip one in reading even his friendliest critics. Robert Conquest, for instance, in the Introduction to *New Lines* (London, 1956), makes a vaguely grateful gesture about the inescapable influence of Auden's 'large and rational talent' and then converts it into a somewhat back-handed compliment when he comments, with apparent complacency, that his anthology has nothing 'of the Auden tendency to turn abstractions into beings in their own right'. The image of solitary man ('man', of course, not 'a man') is a perfect example of this tendency, which depends on insight of heart and mind, and is a tendency to create personifications while staying on the right, the feeling, side of the abstraction. Keats did it too, in 'To Autumn' and the 'Ode to Psyche'.

The separate limb has its individual strength and structure, but it is only a limb. The poet swings back to self, in a private meditation set off by the encounter with miserable age, moving more introvertedly into memory. The activity and sensuousness, the wit and strong climax are left for a flat, subdued style, the style for recollections of winter, failure, and death. As in good conversation poems, the flow and transition are easy and plausible. The old man makes him look back from spring, makes him remember other people who will not be feeling springlike, but 'sorry in this time'. But the poem, because it is a poem, not a conversation, works through a multiplicity of little links: disease, death, failure, collapse of pride, are now presented in another key, quietly and unshockingly, but no less wretchedly, in the reticence of listed particulars:

> The death by cancer of a once hated master,
> A friend's analysis of his own failure,
> Listened to at intervals throughout the winter
> At different hours and in different rooms.
> But always with success of others for comparison.

From this we return again to happiness, courage, nature ('Gerhart Meyer/from the sea') and strength. Even the shift from the anonymity of the death and the failure—'a master' and 'a friend'—plays its part, contrasted with the naming of those whose success makes them nameable. The formal mastery is plain in detail and larger unit, showing itself also, for instance, in the movement of this second stanza, which inverts the first figure.

Later, when we have got to the passage of self-analysis in the second section, we know what the poet is talking about when he claims:

> Coming out of me living is always thinking,
> Thinking changing and changing living,
> Am feeling as it was seeing—
> In city leaning on harbour parapet
> To watch a colony of duck below
> Sit, preen, and doze on buttresses
> Or upright paddle on flickering stream,
> Casually fishing at a passing straw.
> Those find sun's luxury enough,
> Shadow know not of homesick foreigner
> Nor restlessness of intercepted growth.

The poem tells us what it is doing. It is most 'thinking' in the first three lines, but their fluidity hastens us on to the actual conversion of seeing into thinking as the ducks' being is acted on by the human becoming. The seeing becomes part of the feeling as the affectionate appreciation of their life-in-the-moment becomes longing or envy; the feeling becomes part of the thinking in the contrast between the animal sufficiency and the human painful unbeastlike change. It repeats, with a difference, the earlier pattern. The poet is not to the ducks as the solitary man was to the poet: he leans over, but their uprightness, echoing the upright walk through the gardens, is not shadowed by him. Every detail falls resonantly into place: 'shadow' and 'restlessness' work physically and symbolically. And the 'changing' has been demonstrated, in the poem, in the loss of the earlier posture and ease.

In this kind of widening and deepening movement we go on: the swing from inner to outer is a mode of penetration. Through images of seeing and conversions into feeling and thinking, we generalise, take in the outer world and the poet's self-reflection. We take in, among other things, the reduced pared-down account of growth from embryo to adult where all the detail is responsive—'warm in mother' glances back at 'an embryo chicken'; flickers of social detail like 'ancestral property in Wales' which fill in the outer world's class-structure; and the process of the seasons. As it grows more specific about the feeling and the thinking, about fear, isolation, and love, and their problems, the poem grows more specific too about the environment. As in other poems the poet seems to be drawn into the outer world's violence and pity, now by an image, now by a friend's passion:

> Walking home late I listened to a friend
> Talking excitedly of final war
> Of proletariat against police—
> That one shot girl of nineteen through the knees
> They threw that one down concrete stair—
> Till I was angry, said I was pleased.

The poem reveals more geographical and political detail, blending the image and the symbol, until we arrive at the final section which is both highly personal and highly political:

> You whom I gladly walk with, touch,
> Or wait for as one certain of good,

We know it, we know that love
Needs more than the admiring excitement of union,
More than the abrupt self-confident farewell . . .
Needs death, death of the grain, our death,
Death of the old gang.

The sense of the poet's turning to personal address, the poem moving out of meditation into conversation, is a typical Auden movement. We find it sometimes as a modulation from levity into gravity, as in 'The Truest Poetry is the Most Feigning' which shows its hand only after a burlesque and a discussion of feigning. We find it too in 'In Praise of Limestone' where the conclusion sets the nature of personal love—either as there or learned from its absence—against the nature, need, and demands of political action. A perfectly good insight about human love—its demands in union or farewell—and political action—its demands in commitments and sacrifice—are set side by side, and the charm, excitement, and toughness of each admission is increased by the interlocking.

When Richard Ohmann risks the generalisation that Auden's 'interest in leftist reform movements scarcely went beyond their psychological impact on society' (in 'Auden's Sacred Awe', *Commonweal*, lxxviii, May 1963) he is ignoring this and other poems about the relationship of the personal life to political action. The technique of fragmentation and ellipsis allows the poet to subdue, reveal, hide, and leap as he likes. The partly submerged images proceed in this kind of exchange so that what seems to work or not to work in the private life also works or does not work in the social imperative. Neither the private nor the public feeling is instrumentally reduced: they elucidate and respond to each other, in an exchange of metaphor and sensuous force.

III

I want now to move on more quickly to show this combination of interlocked powers at work in several of the best and most difficult poems[1] in *Look, Stranger!* In none of these poems do we end with the

---

[1] The impact and quality of these poems has, as far as I know, only been truly acknowledged by Barbara Everett, in her excellent introduction, *Auden* (London, 1964).

social imperative. In all of them we find the public and private centres
of feeling and their interrelationship. It is sometimes a polarity, sometimes a blurring, of passion and of metaphor. Poem II of *Look, Stranger!*
('A Summer Night, 1933') which Spender says 'possesses a Midsummer
Night's Dream quality which he never achieved before or since' draws
a charmed circle of summer night, warmth, lawn, moonlight, love, and
close fellowship. The poet draws us from time to time outside the
charm, showing its seclusion, its limits, its doom. The qualities within
the circle are beloved, offered up as the necessary sacrifice of love. The
feelings are quite different from those in '1929' where there was a sense
of adult sexual relation, tough, exciting, even brutal; here there is a
rare sweetness, cheerful joy, and a childlike grave simplicity. The
abstractions are delicate nursery beasts, charmed and tamed:

> The lion griefs loped from the shade
> And on our knees their muzzles laid,
>   And Death put down his book.

Love, too, is set down with a quiet-glancing, amorous certainty:

> Moreover, eyes in which I learn
> That I am glad to look, return
>   My glances every day...

The poet uses the clear cool viewpoint of the enchanting moon to
take us beyond the circle, outside the creepered walls to central Europe
and to the nearer multitudes 'whose glances hunger worsens'. (The echo
of the earlier amorous glances here is a fine effect lost in the revised version where stanza five is cut out.) There is no personal movement from
private to public experience, but a bird's-eye or moon's-eye view of the
precarious shut-off innocence, cultivated delights and the threat beyond. In his *Spring Symphony* Benjamin Britten responds wonderfully
to the turn in the poem, which comes halfway through, in a crossing of
private and public metaphor. We exchange the metaphor taken by
lascivious love from politics for the unmetaphoric bare source, moving
from 'With a sigh endure/The tyrannies of love' at the end of one
stanza to 'And, gentle, do not care to know/Where Poland draws her
Eastern bow/What violence is done.' Britten's crashing brass only falls
during those last two lines, to return from terror to languorous sweetness, marking the poem's withdrawal to a pleasure in endurance and
tyranny. The music, like the poem, has a plaintive sweetness. The poem

is grave, not ironic, and even its end, foreseeing the destruction of the charmed circle, has a high note of joyous sacrifice:

> As through a child's rash happy cries
> The drowned voice of his parents rise
> In unlamenting song.

Perhaps the Midsummer Night's Dream was unique in Auden. The discursive conversation-like form allows him to treat the theme flexibly and more complexly in three very fine poems of love and politics: 'The Malverns' ('Here on the cropped grass'), 'Two Worlds' ('The chimneys are smoking') and 'A Bride in the 30's' ('Easily, my dear, you move'). In all three the languages of love and war and politics are crossed and interchanged in a pattern of covert, even furtive, cross-questioning. In 'Here on the cropped grass' the lover's absence is the occasion of the social vision and imperative. Love had ignored the world outside: 'Business shivered in a banker's winter/While we were kissing'. When the kissing stopped the poet looked beyond, at the children, the cramped clerk, the little men and their mothers, the 'luxury liner' of the cathedral (direct hit by metaphor) filled with the 'high thin rare continuous worship of the self-absorbed'. The illustrations of the human condition are smaller and more abstract, the view more remote, than in '1929' but the same enlargement is there. The thunder speaks in this poem, and though its message is not that of T. S. Eliot's thunder, it is talking about waste, economic and moral. At times the private and the public speak with one voice, from the same confused, depressed doubt:

> And England to our meditations seemed
>   The perfect setting:
> But now it has no innocence at all;
> It is the isolation and the fear,
>   The mood itself;
> It is the body of the absent lover,
> An image to the would-be hero of the soul,
> The little area we are willing to forgive
>   Upon conditions.

Or, 'For private reasons I must have the truth'. Here there is a true and rare double entendre in which the words, as in a pun, make distinct sense in two separate ways. Later, the amorous language is metaphorically subdued to the political feeling, but the earlier personal address and duality give an ironic undertone:

> The relations of your lovers were, alas, pictorial;
> The treasure that you stole, you lost; bad luck
> It brought you, but you cannot put it back
>   Now with caresses.

And

> Has not your long affair with death
> Of late become increasingly more serious;
>   Do you not find
> Him growing more attractive every day?

And, at the end,

> These moods give no permission to be idle,
> For men are changed by what they do;
> And through loss and anger the hands of the unlucky
>   Love one another.

At times it is a genuine double subject, though one mood colours both. At times the initial subject of love offers its source of metaphor. At times the poem's enigmatic cutting makes it look as if what the poet learns from love can teach him about society, about change in action, about superficiality, about loss. Or is it, the poem's covertness then makes us ask, that what we see in the desperate lives around reflects back after all on our loving?

'The chimneys are smoking' is grander, calmer, more exhilarated, though at times sinister and covert. The parted lovers are there, so is the solitude of the hawk's view, and the look beyond self and personal love to the public life. Love and politics are conflated and confused in the image of the game between the Whites and Reds, for the 'game . . . which tends to become like a war' is both politics and love. The lovers are given pieces that fit, 'Whereat with love we trembled'. The mood is one of longing and exultation, than takes on a grave sublimity in its enlargement:

> We ride a turning globe, we stand on a star;
> It has thrust us up together; it is stronger than we.
> In it our separate sorrows are a single hope,
>   It's in its nature always to appear
>   Behind us as we move
>   With linked arms through our dreams,
>   Wherefore, apart, we love
>   Its sundering streams.

The image of political union is at once a symbol and an actual reflection of their relationship and their belief. Here there is an effective clandestine suggestiveness which fits both the love and the political action:

> And since our desire cannot take that route which is straightest,
> Let us choose the crooked, so implicating these acres,
> These millions in whom already the wish to be one
>> Like a burglar is stealthily moving,
>> That these, on the new façade of a bank
>> Employed, or conferring at health resort,
>> May, by cirumstance linked,
>> More clearly act our thought.

The concluding feeling of a joy both secret and abounding, has a vitality that also fits the private and the public feeling. These two extraordinary poems, oddly neglected in Auden criticism, suggest ways perhaps in which you work from the known to the imagined in 'entertaining' belief. They also create cryptic allegories, like those of Rex Warner, in which the element of mystery is as conspicuous as the element of clarity. The blurred or confused association is a useful cover, a way of writing enigmatic poetry of love or politics or both.

'Easily, my dear, you move' begins by setting both the private and the public images together in the conceit of a photographer's album. The poem is partly concerned with the irony of taking the public life as a mere ground for the private love. There is the recurring point that love can be enclosed, innocent or ruthless, in spite of the public life, ignoring its imperatives: 'In the policed unlucky city/Lucky his bed', and 'He from these lands of terrifying mottoes/Makes worlds as innocent as Beatrix Potter's'. Through a striking use of a metaphor which was later to become a central symbol in wartime poetry—the dance— the poem begins to argue that there are some images that cannot be ignored or absorbed:

> Summoned by such a music from our time,
> Such images to audience come
> As vanity cannot dispel nor bless:

and we move from a relativist, pictorial flick-through of the imagery of the personal relation to the imperatives:

> Hunger and love in their variations
> Grouped invalids watching the flight of the birds
> And single assassins.

The poem also makes explicit a connection between private and public experience: 'But love, except at our proposal/Will do no trick at his disposal' . . . 'and through our private stuff must work/His public spirit'. The poem proceeds to argue, in an irony and appeal not unlike Shakespeare's in the sonnets, that love is open to special ruthless temptation:

> Be deaf too, standing uncertain now,
> A pine tree shadow across your brow,
> To what I hear and wish I did not;
> The voice of love saying lightly, brightly—
> 'Be Lubbe, Be Hitler, but be my good
> Daily, nightly.'

The moral choice that confronts the beautiful and the beloved is indicated only as a general moral choice, no details specified. But though the poem is an obscure one, it manages to move on its substantial public images. The images of mad, laughing Lubbe (blamed for the Reichstag fire) and of Hitler are carriers of violent repulsion and power. The feeling of the public imagery makes the feeling in the private affair plain. It is substantial enough to be there in its own right, without any air of existing just as symbol, though it makes a very reticent and furtive treatment of the personal subject, just viable. As in all the poems I have been discussing, there is an undercurrent of the clandestine excitement that moves over easily from love to politics. Any discussion of love and Love must note, incidentally, that the enlargement does not invariably work from love's goodness to Love's Goodness. The morality and passions of the private and the public subjects, at work in the poetry, are visibly subtle and complex. When Auden praised Henry James's mastery of 'nuance and scruple', he knew what he was talking about.

IV

These are poems of the thirties. What happens to this association of the private and public worlds when the poetry becomes Christian, and steadily more anti-political? I think the emblem of the face and the map still fits, even though the associations cease to be so covert and obscure.

There are poems where Auden seems to need to be reticent about religion, as he was about politics, and always had been about love. There are also a number of poems where the religious or social sense is posed against, or joined with, the sense of personal experience. In one of his most successful religious poems, 'In Sickness and in Health' (from *Collected Shorter Poems*), there is another explicit discussion of the relation between the individual act and the larger vision, which is no longer a social imperative, but the idea of God. We move again from love to Love, and the poem achieves images for both, and indeed discusses the need to begin with the human particular:

> Let none say I Love until aware
> What huge resources it will take to nurse
> One ruining speck, one tiny hair

It begins to be apparent, in the poetry of the forties, that the inner and outer experiences have to be connected: Auden's religious poetry, unlike Eliot's or Vaughan's, stays in time. In this poem the religious feeling which Auden has been accused of lacking (by G. S. Fraser, for one) is first carried by and then seems to blossom out of a sustained affectionate personal address:

> Beloved, we are always in the wrong,
> Handling so clumsily our stupid lives,
>   Suffering too little or too long,
>   Too careful even in our selfish loves:
> The decorative manias we obey
> Die in grimaces round us every day,
> Yet through their tohu-bohu comes a voice
> Which utters an absurd command—Rejoice.

The affection, gravely reasoning tone, slightly toughened by irony, but not to the point of defensive erosion, is absolutely right for putting the Absurd command, and for respecting it. Auden then manages a marvellous modulation out of the personal, by the bridge-passage of a prayer within a prayer:

> ... beloved, pray
> That Love, to Whom necessity is play,
> Do what we must yet cannot do alone
> And lay your solitude beside my own.[1]

---

[1] Since writing this I have discovered that Auden deleted the stanza for the 1966 edition, but my view of its power is unchanged.

It moves us beyond:

> Force our desire, O Essence of creation,
> To seek Thee always in Thy substances.

To this imperative we come through a conflation of feeling (quite right), a slow approach (also right), and a tentative exchange of languages, through the known and familiar human love to Love. The movement out of the substances towards 'Essence of Creation' is right because it proves the whole point about seeking through the substances.

The movement, as in the political poetry, is not always in one direction, and we move naturally enough back into the personal sense. This is what happens, for instance, at the end of 'In Praise of Limestone'. His love poetry, simple or complex, is surely rare in the honesty, toughness, and delicacy in which it makes the most of small-scale experience, and the low claims he makes for human experience, while not losing value of dignity or respect, have an important part to play in his religious feeling. But that is to touch on another subject.

The religious poetry does not move only between the poles of love and Love. In 'Memorial for the City', for instance, from *Nones*, we move from a brilliantly managed but necessarily abstract survey of the history of the City to a final abstract voice that speaks for human weakness, for the Flesh. It is a highly personal point of repose, though a personification, and one presented through a composite response to myth and history and literature:

> I heard Orpheus sing; I was not quite as moved as they say.
> I was not taken in by the sheep's-eyes of Narcissus; I was angry
>   with Psyche when she struck a light.
> I was in Hector's confidence; so far as it went.
> Had he listened to me Oedipus would never have left Corinth; I
>   cast no vote at the trial of Orestes.
> I fell asleep when Diotima spoke of love; I was not responsible
>   for the monsters which tempted St Anthony.
> To me the Saviour permitted His Fifth Word from the cross; to
>   be a stumbling block to the stoics.
> I was the unwelcome third of the meetings of Tristan with Isolda;
>   they tried to poison me.
> I rode with Galahad on his Quest for the San Graal; without
>   understanding I kept his vow.

I was the just impediment to the marriages of Faustus with
  Helen; I know a ghost when I see one.
With Hamlet I had no patience; but I forgave Don Quixote all
  for his admission in the cart.

Strictly speaking, this dramatised voice does not find a place in my
argument, since it is generalised and abstract. I want to include it as a
splendid example of an abstraction that after all presents a personal
standpoint of feeling, because of its easy moving, colloquial, but cumu-
latively very formalised prosaic language, because of its personal sounding intelligence and warmth, and because of the effect of the particulars
and their humanity. We have to work to appreciate this voice: why
can he be bored by Orpheus, disapprove of Ahab, and yet ride with
Galahad? Why is his relationship with Orpheus and Hector restricted?
Why feel impatient with Hamlet *and* Psyche? And so on. The deceptive
obviousness of the list, like its deceptive casualness, engages us, but the
engagement wouldn't work if it were not for the unity of personality.
We may respond to the list as to a quiz, but the sense of character makes
the riddles animated and coherent. The speech resembles the conversation of good friends, allusive, easy, combining intimate warmth with
the charm of the myths themselves and their personality. The Voice
and the inhabitants of his anthology have substance. Indeed, every
detail has a dramatised inflection that is highly individual: it is a voice
speaking to us, familiarly and knowingly. It is unsophisticated but not
as naïve as you might expect; consistent and candid but not transparent;
at times firm—'I know a ghost when I see one'—at times vaguer—
'without understanding', always so subtly witty that the wit's action
tends to be a little delayed. Auden at his most grave and at his most
entertaining.
  A not dissimilar voice comes through when he identifies Clio in the
fine title poem of *Homage to Clio*, where the abstraction is precisely
what humanises and particularises a poem of conceptual generality.
Again, the substances are needed by the concept, the public image is
made up of private ones. Though the poet asks, 'How shall I describe
you?' this is not a dry mock at the difficulties of addressing the ineffable.
Clio is human, individual, Muse of the unique event:

> ... what icon
> Have the arts for you, who look like any

> Girl one has not noticed and show no special
>> Affinity with a beast? I have seen
> Your photo, I think, in the papers, nursing
>> A baby or mourning a corpse: each time
>
> You had nothing to say and did not, one could see,
>> Observe where you were. . .

Here the personal voice is the poet's voice of appropriate feeling: there is too much respect for more than a little compassion, there is a loving and proper knowingness, and at the end he can even risk an affectionate conceit, about himself as well as Clio:

> I dare not ask you if you bless the poets,
> For you do not look as if you ever read them
> Nor can I see a reason why you should.

V

Auden's smaller and simpler poems may catch a resonance from the habitual neighbourhood of this kind of poetry. Most of his love poems and his religious poems depend on the shadow, if not the substance, of a larger reference. And some of his smaller poems have something of the scale and complexity of those I have been talking about. 'Prime', for instance, is a short lyric which has a map and a face, and wakes to appreciate its rich possessions:

> And I know that I am, here, not alone
>> But with a world, and rejoice
> Unvexed, for the will has still to claim
>> This adjacent arm as my own.
> The memory to name me, resume
>> Its routine of praise and blame,
> And smiling to me is this instant while
>> Still the day is intact, and I
> The Adam sinless in our beginning,
>> Adam still previous to any act.
>
> I draw breath; that is of course to wish
>> No matter what to be wise,

To be different to die and the cost
    No matter how is Paradise
Lost of course and myself owing a death:
    The eager ridge, the steady sea,
The flat roofs of the fishing village
    Still asleep in its bunny,
Though as fresh and sunny still are not friends
    But things to hand, this ready flesh
No honest equal, but my accomplice now
    My assassin to be and my name
Stands for my historical share of care
    For a lying self-made city,
Afraid of our living task, the dying
    Which the coming day will ask.

8

The Personal and the Impersonal in some of Dylan Thomas's Lyrics

Lyric poetry attaches personal experience to the world outside, colouring events and ideas with individual passion, or transmuting particulars into symbol and metaphor. Most lyric poems involve some shift from the particular to the general, from the bed of sleeping love to the meditation on Love's aspiration and weakness, from a crowd on London Bridge to the sense of modern devastation, from real friends and lovers to the value of community, from a rising to thoughts of violence and honour, from stooks tossed by wind to God's grandeur, from birds, beasts, and flowers to the sense of sexuality and individuality. A starry night, a fog, or sunlight on a garden provide the occasion and the image for meditation, and offer the reader familiar surfaces and points of entry. There are occasions when the lyric poems of Dylan Thomas show something of this shift and conjunction, but it is often absent, or seems to be absent. He sometimes seems to dispense with the surface of personal and particular occasion, offering a severe though sensuously brilliant abstract imagery or drama. The high degree of impersonality, or apparent impersonality, is a cause or an effect of Thomas's surrealism, his oddity, and his obscurity. It is hard to think of any other poet of his time who writes so abstractedly and impersonally about love and friendship, topical events, daily life. Nearly all the things, events and people found in his stories, and in *Under Milk Wood*, are conspicuously absent in his poems, or present in a curiously subdued or suppressed way.

'After the Funeral' belongs quite clearly to the world of stories and plays, and has a personal point of view, an eye and an 'I', a real and named heroine, Ann Jones, and a rich drama of social occasion. There are objects like a stuffed fox and a fern, and amusing if unsympathetically drawn mourners at the funeral, with their 'mule praises, brays/ Windshake of sail-shaped ears' and grotesque and funereal eyes and teeth. The 'I' of the poem seems to be the most serious mourner, but he is criticised for a bardic swell which makes 'a monstrous image blindly/ Magnified out of praise'. The imagery is in fact anything but blindly magnified, and he trips it up before it gets started, in order to set it scrupulously and defensively on its feet. In order to be about Ann, it has also to be about itself, and he praises her both by denying the appropriateness of the praise, for such a meek woman, and then by swelling its licensed hyperbole. The poem's unusually wide field of emotional detail, about false and true mourning, hard religion, dusty and narrow parlour life, hard kitchen drudgery, and pain, is eventually channelled into the praise, which ruefully but tenderly deprecates its own windiness. Its image of marble is right for its compensating grandeur, for its hardness, for its constriction and arduousness, while the breaking of chapel confines is also right for such virtue. The local transformations too are just right, that religious and arthritic cramp repeated in the stone, the sudsoaked old hands now sublimely 'cloud-sopped'. The parlour ornaments of dead nature and domestic propriety are invoked for the imagined resurrection at the end,

> Storm me forever over her grave until
> The stuffed lung of the fox twitch and cry Love
> And the strutting fern lay seeds on the black sill.

The poem is in command of its own rhetoric, has a lucid narrative line, which makes scene and feelings plain, and manages to unify a variety of tones and details. But it is perhaps slightly awkward in the transition from poet to Ann, and back again, raising the question of decorum without doing anything about it. And it seems to break out in the last three lines into something more interesting and urgent still, in its Stanley Spencer-like combination of the domestic and the visionary for a precisely imagined resurrection. A similar awkwardness and disproportion occurs in 'A Refusal to Mourn the Death, by Fire, of a Child in London', which seems rather obscurely to join elegy with an attempt to shy away from elegy, on similar grounds of inappropriateness. But whatever Thomas has in mind by the possibility of murdering 'The mankind of her going with a grave truth'—is it a refusal to lament, or to lament conventionally?—his poem does seem to do what he seems to be trying not to do. This lyric also seems to move away from the thought of the child, and the air-raid, to a splendid invocation of that death into nature which is Thomas's theme and consolation in so many

poems, and which doesn't seem to emerge quite lucidly from the particulars of the death.

The same odd dislocation—rather more than slight, in this case—
comes about in 'Over Sir John's Hill'. Most of the poem is taken up
with a playful, witty and clever imposition of fable on to landscape
and natural happening, in which animals, landscape, and sea are appor-
tioned roles in a story of murder, trial, execution, requiem, and divine
forgiveness. The parts and roles sit lightly on the scene, sometimes
seeming to fit perfectly, as with the murderous hawk and priestlike
heron, then blurring into multiple action, so that the hawk is not only
murderer but executioner, the little birds guilty as well as victims, the
heron a killer too. And the hill dons the black cap of judgment in an
agreeably arbitrary visual conceit as the birds darken its summit. But
the clever allegory of a nature red in tooth and claw does not seem quite
to make a poem, despite some good local strokes of wit, like the gulled
birds 'haring' or the 'hawk-eyed dusk', which take us back to origins
of metaphor in a way that underlines the generalisation and the fable.
It has not much feeling, except for certain local exceptions, like seeing
death plain in a shell, or invoking God's pity on the birds 'for their
breast of whistles'. But the poem ends with calm melancholy, largely
inhering in a sense of solitary, elegiac mournful music, in which heron,
poet, and the sounds and sights of evening join in sad orchestration.
That final haunting sorrowfulness seems an inexplicable movement
away from the brilliant morality play, moving in an unforeseen and
more profound stream of feeling. The poem might well be neatly
analysed in terms of Thomas's famous (and limited) formula of the
dialectic war and peace of images, but if we come to follow its track of
feeling, that final movement seems to sweep us into a new world of
feeling.

These three poems, 'After the Funeral', 'A Refusal to Mourn' and
'Over Sir John's Hill' show an imbalance of the narrative and the feeling
in late developments which seem to extend the poem disconcertingly,
uncertainly locating point, purpose, and passion. Each poem is about
some other life, human or natural, but also needs a self-conscious
signature by the poet or fabulist, which may perhaps offer some clue
to the dislocations of feeling. We might put the matter more simply,
however, and see in Thomas an inability to break away from his
obsessions, a strong undertow working in the poems, against the flow
of the overt theme or situation. Something like this may be happening

in that dialogue between mother and unborn child, 'If my head hurt a hair's foot', where the beginning invokes powerfully humane feelings of tenderness, solicitude, and courage, but leads in the end to one more vision of deadly genesis, life as death. The images at the beginning are realistically emotional and physical, in 'iron head', 'bunched monkey coming'; and the pun, 'The bed is a cross place' endows one of Thomas's favourite pieces of wordplay with a simple, playful, wide-eyed childish innocence. There is a delicate sense of imagined fear and risk, and a parental attempt to imagine the unborn but live creature with tenderness, solicitude, and apprehension. The mother here is very unlike the mother in Sylvia Plath's poem, 'Nick and the Candlestick', where the world that is feared for the child is the precisely poisoned world of an actual environment. Here the mother's voice takes on the passionate but impersonal hectoring of so many Thomas poems, to insist that the child must be 'bounced from a good home' to the morbid life-cycle and then the natural death-cycle:

> Rest beyond choice in the dust-appointed grain,
> At the breast stored with seas. No return
> Through the waves of the fat streets nor the skeleton's thin ways.
> The grave and my calm body are shut to your coming as stone.
> And the endless beginning of prodigies suffers open.

Once more, Thomas seems to go beyond the expected abstraction, into a recurring vision of genesis and dying. We may complain of a too predictable conclusion, and a weight of abstraction which swallows up, rather than matches, the human particular. But there are of course many poems where Thomas does not start with such particular dramas and images, but creates his vitality entirely out of abstract images and ideas, as in the entirely successful, 'The force that through the green fuse drives the flower'. Here, too, there is the self-consciousness about writing poetry, taking the form of a lament that he cannot express his affinity with that world of nature where he is so utterly at one with vegetation, rocks, wind and water.

The puzzle about why we write gets into 'After the Funeral', 'A Refusal to Mourn' and 'Over Sir John's Hill' in a slightly dislocated fashion, but in this poem it takes its place centrally and confidently, and I don't think it strikes us as odd unless we scrutinise it in critical cold-blood. We may well wonder a little about the need so violently to lament the lack of communication between poet and his fellow nature, his numbness and its deafness, for though one could imagine a Franciscan poem about the sadness of not writing poetry for brother water and sister flower, this is not it. But what it most urgently laments, as in all the other poems I have been discussing, is our shared mortality, and our shared energy. Thomas is here entirely concerned with showing the combination of genesis and death, vitality and morbidity, and does so through his genius for language and his extraordinary imagination of nature. The word 'fuse' does marvellously for explosive charge and flower-stem, and makes the brilliant appearance of flower continue the metaphor with powerful implicitness. Slightly more obviously and analytically, the common needs of love-beds and coffins for sheets, and the conjunction of wormlike penis with penislike shapes and shifts of worms, make sex and death join grimly, uncomfortably, but stoically. All the same, the very thought of Marvell's rather different sexy worms reminds us of Thomas's strange and typical lack of an imagined or imputed listener. The poem is written as if it were indeed addressed to vegetation, wind and water.

And successfully so addressed. Thomas was published in Roger Roughton's surrealist *Contemporary Verse* and his early poems have something in common with the poetry of Barker and Gascoyne, though these two contemporary surrealist poets are more lucidly personal and less conceptual than Thomas. 'The force that through the green fuse' shows a true surrealist gift for linking the human world with the natural, giving a grotesque life to abstraction by granting it the human lineaments of disembodied mouth and hand, and approximating human vitality to abstraction by imagining the common action of stirring hand and sucking mouth at work on springs and veins. The generalisations of 'My youth' are given a particular shape by these thoroughly imagined conceits of a partially—only partially—anthropomorphised nature. Nature becomes more human, human life more elemental. The result is much more lively and powerful than the charming intricacies of 'Over Sir John's Hill', though the ease with which Thomas's fantasy becomes arch doesn't always make it easy to say when his imagination is working at high pressure, when at low.

In one of his best poems, 'Do not go gentle into that good night', we see again that Thomas's passionately felt particulars are not visible as detailed cases of personal situation and character, but are ground small, grist to his very special mill. The playfulness of this poem is totally and tenderly bent to its end of sadness and energetic exhortation.

Here at last we find the insistence on the morbidity of genesis transformed to an energetic way of dying. The anger and grief are there,
visibly, for 'my father', but the passionate argument is conducted
through abstractions, in the generalised cases of the deaths and lives of
wise men, good men, wild men and grave men. It is through their
examples, dazzlingly invoked, that the elegy proceeds, to make the case
for the father's refusal to die gently too. The poem is about old age,
about death, about the incompleteness of all living, however directed.
The poem is wild and grave, furious and sad, and the imagined lives,
the wordplay and the villanelle's sway from imperative to indicative
mood, always brought back to the inexorable refrain, create a great
elegy. The final moving image of elevation, remoteness, and separat-
tion, 'And you, my father, there on the sad height' completes and
transforms the play of abstraction in a sudden, brief, release of personal
address. There are many poems where the personal is never even implicitly present, where legend and myth makes the whole life of narrative and feeling. In these poems, as in the ones I have been discussing,
it is important to applaud Thomas's sensuous power, because his
abstractions are never coldly and intellectually presented, but always
dynamic, exciting and thoroughly sensed. In the powerful poem about
war and annunciations, 'Into her lying down head' we find Thomas's
surrealist fantasy, in 'Whales unreined from the green grave/In foun-
tains of origin gave up their love' and the passionate and perceptive
literary allusions to 'Juan aflame and savagely young King Lear', which
show different ways of animating abstraction and myth. There is
something like Blake's power to imagine the inanimate life in 'Two
sand grains together in bed/Head to heaven-circling head' and Yeats's
command of sexualised mythology in the very Yeats-like annunciations
of:

> A she bird sleeping brittle by
> Her lover's wings that fold tomorrow's flight,
>> Within the nested treefork
>> Sings to the treading hawk
> Carrion, paradise, chirrup my bright yolk

The abstractions of myth are characterised, given feeling and endowed
with sensuous life. Other instances that come to mind are the coupling
of bird and woman at the end of 'A Winter's Tale' where the images of
'whirlpool at the wanting centre' and the 'rose with him flowering in

her melting snow' are just right for the annunciation which is re-
enacted myth, and for a winter tale of sexual consummation. The same
power to create the life of abstractions is there in the rush and vertigin-
ous, heady motion of 'Fern Hill'—'the owls were bearing the farm
away' makes us feel that intoxication of sleepy, drunken, lovely youth,
and the rendering of its colours, 'fire green as grass' and all the violently
stripped visual images make us remember the primitive child's vision.
The surrealist painter Thomas most resembles is surely Chagall, who
shares the romantic nostalgia, the swimminess, the naïf child's vision,
the combinations of abstract and grotesque conceits, the sexuality, and the rhapsodic feeling for nature. Chagall's brilliance of
colour is also matched, in another medium, by Thomas, for the colour
of his abstract sayings is by no means the least important source of
animation. There are all the recurrences of his brilliant and many toned
greens. Green shines in one animated abstract image which relives
Edenic creation in a tender, affectionate, bright beauty:

> And then to awake, and the farm, like a wanderer white
> With the dew, come back, the cock on his shoulder: it was all
> 　Shining, it was Adam and maiden,
> 　　The sky gathered again
> 　And the sun grew round that very day.
> So it must have been after the birth of the simple light
> In the first, spinning place, the spellbound horses walking warm
> 　Out of the whinnying green stable
> 　　On to the fields of praise.

Such lines, and such poems, show that Thomas felt an affinity with the
natural world which enabled him truly to imagine what Wordsworth
calls the life of things, to see the farm lovingly, amusingly and precisely as a wanderer with a cock perched on his shoulder, to imagine
the warmth, strangeness, and newness of Adam's stable.

'Fern Hill' and 'Poem in October' succeed in writing Thomas's
usual story of life and death in a thorough and radiant imagining of life,
where the sense of admiration and love is unmistakably personal. This
is a love-poetry for nature. Thomas does occasionally write more
successful love-poetry about the human world than either 'After the
funeral' or 'If my head' or even 'Do not go gentle'. There are two
poems which seem to me triumphs of a personally imagined idea, 'The
Conversation of Prayer' and 'The Hunchback in the Park'. Each is

marked by a strong and clearly visible narrative column, and their stories are so lucid as to make paraphrase both easy and unnecessary. 'The Conversation of Prayer' is in a sense a highly abstract verse, but despite its allegorical drama of the exchange of prayer and answer, its strength lies in its invocation of occasions of strong feeling. Feeling is severed from cause, in the reticence and brevity of the narrative, which permits us only to know that both boy and man are going to bed, that one simply prays the common childhood prayer for a night without nightmare, and the other for his love to stay alive. It is also arbitrarily severed from cause, and given the force of unexpected climax, by the transfer. The boy is dragged into the ferocious causeless nightmare, the more frightening for being coloured by an adult experience he hasn't yet felt in his life, and the man is graced by an unexpected reprieve, 'no dying but alive and warm/In the fire of his care his love in the high room'. Here the power of emotional experience belongs to everyday and everynight life, but Thomas presents the drama abstractly, mysteriously, and inexplicably. His most realistic love-poem depends on a high degree of abstraction, and a refusal to tell much of the story.

'The Hunchback in the Park' is everyone's most accessible Thomas poem, but less simple and nostalgically narrative than it looks. He sees the park as a refuge for the derelict life and the playground for happiness. The derelict hunchback, who has nowhere else to go, shares with the playing boys a creative impulse. This poem, like so many of the others, is about making, about making something that will last through a longer night than the time between the closing and opening of the park. The park is full of mime, and makebelieve, from the boys' cruel imitations of the hunchback, 'hunchbacked in mockery', to the games of tigers and sailors. Delicately, letting the pressures of making accumulate most naturalistically, the poet moves from the children's playful making to the life-and-death imagination of the hunchback, disfigured, mocked, pushed around, but with an intensely active inner life. He makes, as we all do, in order to have what he cannot ever have, a desirable and beautiful woman. He makes, as we all do, to compensate for defect and correct deformity, a straight and perfect human image. He makes, as we all do, something which will leave a trace out there, which will stay in the park and the dark when he has to go. Perhaps the poem says that we all create, and out of many impulses. Perhaps it says that we need to be derelict and wounded in order to make a perfect

9

The Poetry of Sylvia Plath

I

Passions of hate and horror prevail in the poetry of Sylvia Plath, running strongly counter to the affirmative and life-enhancing quality of most great English poetry, even in this century. We cannot reconcile her despairing and painful protest with the usual ideological demands of Christian, Marxist, and humanist writers, whether nobly and sympathetically eloquent, like Wordsworth, breezily simplified, like Dylan Thomas, or cunning in ethical and psychological argument, like W. H. Auden or F. R. Leavis. Her poetry rejects instead of accepting, despairs instead of glorying, turns its face with steady consistency towards death, not life. But these hating and horrified passions are rooted in love, are rational as well as irrational, lucid as well as bewildered, so humane and honourable that they are constantly enlarged and expanded. We are never enclosed in a private sickness here, and if derangement is a feature of the poetry, it works to enlarge and generalise, not to create an enclosure. Moreover, its enlargment works through passionate reasoning, argument and wit. Its judgment is equal to its genius.

The personal presence in the poetry, though dynamic and shifting, makes itself felt in a full and large sense, in feeling, thinking and language. In view of certain tendencies to admire or reject her so-called derangement as a revelatory or an enclosed self-exploration, I want to stress this breadth and completeness. The poetry constantly breaks beyond its own personal cries of pain and horror, in ways more sane than mad, enlarging and generalising the particulars, attaching its maladies to a profoundly moved and moving sense of human ills. Working through a number of individual poems, I should like to describe this poetry as a poetry of enlargement, not derangement. In much of the poetry the derangement is scarcely present, but where it is, it is out-turned, working though reason and love.

I want to disagree with David Holbrook's view that hers is a schizophrenic poetry which 'involves us in false solutions and even the *huis clos* circuits of death', while indeed agreeing with much that he has to say about the cult of schizophrenia in his essay 'The 200-inch distorting mirror' (*New Society*, 11 July 1968).

Sylvia Plath's poetry demands a selfless mirror-role from us; we feel that it would be worse than inhuman of us not to give it. If this involves us in entering into her own distorted view of existence, never mind. We will bravely become the schizoid's 200-inch astronomical reflector.

An excessive love for the cult of pain and dying, in such tributes as those of Anne Sexton[1] and Robert Lowell,[2] seems to divert our attention from the breadth and rationality of Sylvia Plath's art. Lowell is strongly drawn to that very quality which David Holbrook finds repulsive or pathetic, the invitation to a deadly closure:

> There is a peculiar, haunting challenge to these poems. Probably many, after reading *Ariel*, will recoil from their first over-awed shock, and painfully wonder why so much of it leaves them feeling empty, evasive and inarticulate. In her lines, I often hear the serpent whisper, 'Come, if only you had the courage, you too could have my rightness, audacity and ease of inspiration.' But most of us will turn back. These poems are playing Russian roulette with six cartridges in the cylinder, a game of 'chicken', the wheels of both cars locked and unable to swerve.

It seems worth recording a different reaction.

I want to begin by looking at a poem from *Ariel* which shows how dangerous it is to talk, as Holbrook clearly does, and as Lowell seems to, about the 'typical' Sylvia Plath poem, or even the 'typical' late poem. I must make it clear that I do not want to rest my case on the occasional presence of life-enhancing poems, but to use one to explain what I mean by imaginative enlargement. 'Nick and the Candlestick' (from *Ariel*, 1965; written October/November 1962) is not only a remarkable poem of love, but that much rarer thing—are there any others?—a fine poem of maternal love. It is a poem which moves towards two high points of feeling, strongly personal and particular, deeply eloquent of maternal feeling, and lucidly open to a Christian

---

[1] 'The Barfly Ought to Sing' *Triquarterly*, no. 7, Fall 1966. Reproduced in *The Art of Sylvia Plath*, ed. Charles Newman (London, 1970).

[2] Introduction to *Ariel* (New York, 1966). Republished in *New York Review of Books*, vol. 6, no. 8, 12 March 1966.

mythical enlargement. The first peak comes in the tenth stanza, and can perhaps be identified at its highest point in one word, the endearment 'ruby', which is novel, surprising, resonant, and beautiful:

> Remembering, even in sleep,
> Your crossed position.
> The blood blooms clean
>
> In you, ruby.
> The pain
> You wake to is not yours.

The second peak comes at the end, in a strongly transforming conclusion, a climax in the very last line. It comes right out of all that has been happening in the poem but transforms what has gone before, carrying a great weight and responsibility, powerfully charged and completing a process, like an explosion or a blossoming:

> You are the one
> Solid the spaces lean on, envious.
> You are the baby in the barn.

The final enlargement is daring, both in the shock of expansion and in the actual claim it makes. She dares to call her baby Christ and in doing so makes the utmost claim of her personal love, but so that the enlargement does not take us away from this mother, this child, this feeling. This most personally present mother-love moves from the customary hyperbole of endearment in 'ruby' to the vast claim. When we look back, when we read again, the whole poem is pushing towards that last line, 'You are the baby in the barn'. The symbol holds good, though at first invisibly, for the cold, the exposure, the dark, the child, the mother, the protection, and the redemption from a share of pain. Each sensuous and emotional step holds for the mother in the poem and for Mary: this is the warmth of the mother nursing her child in the cold night; this is a proud claim for the child's beauty and the mother's tenderness; this is love and praise qualified by pain. Any mother loving her child in a full awareness of the world's horror—especially seeing it and feeling it vulnerable and momentarily safe in sleep—is re-enacting the feeling in the Nativity, has a right to call the child the baby in the barn.

'Ruby' is a flash of strong feeling. It treasures, values, praises, admires, measures, contemplates, compares, rewards. Its full stretch of passion is only apparent when the whole poem is read, but even on first encounter it makes a powerful moment, and strikes us as thoroughly formed and justified at that stage. Like every part of the poem, even the less urgent-sounding ones, it refers back and forwards, and has also continuity not only within the poem but with larger traditions of amorous and religious language, in medieval poetry (especially *The Pearl*), in the Bible, in Hopkins. The fusion of the new and the old is moving. This baby has to be newly named, like every baby, and has its christening in a poem, which bestows a unique name, in creative energy, as ordinary christenings cannot, but with something too of the ritual sense of an old and common feeling. Sylvia Plath is a master of timing and placing, and the naming endearment comes after the physically live sense of the sleeping child, in the cold air, in the candlelight, in its healthy colour. The mildly touched Christian reference in 'crossed position' prepares for the poem's future. Its gentleness contrasts strongly, by the way, with the violence of very similar puns in Dylan Thomas, and confirms my general feeling that Sylvia Plath is one of the very few poets to assimilate Thomas without injury, in an entirely benign influence. Her sensuous precision is miles away from Thomas: 'ruby' is established by the observation, 'The blood blooms clean/In you', and the comparison works absolutely, within the poem, though it has an especially poignant interest when we think of the usual aggressiveness and disturbance of redness in her other poems, where the blooming red of tulips or poppies are exhausting life-demands, associated with the pain of red wounds, or the heavy urgency of a surviving beating heart. Here it is a beloved colour, because it is the child's, so in fact there is a constancy of symbolism, if we are interested. 'Clean', like 'crossed' and 'ruby' has the same perfectly balanced attachment to the particularity of the situation—this mother, this baby—and to the Christian extension. 'The pain/You wake to is not yours' works in the same way, pointing out and in, though the words 'out' and 'in' do less than justice to the fusion here.

The perfected fusion is the more remarkable for being worked out in a complex tone, which includes joking. Like the medieval church, or the Nativity play, it can be irreverent, can make jokes about what it holds sacred, is sufficiently inclusive and sufficiently certain. So we are carried from the fanciful rueful joke about 'A piranha/Religion, drinking/Its first communion out of my live toes' to the final awe. Or from the casual profane protest, 'Christ! they are panes of ice' to the crossed position, the pain not his, the baby in the barn. An ancient and audacious range.

If this is a love-poem, it is one which exists in the context of the other *Ariel* poems, keeping a sense of terrors as well as glories, in imagery which is vast and vague: the stars 'plummet to their dark address'; and topically precise and scientific: 'the mercuric/Atoms that cripple drip/ Into the terrible well'. It is a poisoned world that nourishes and threatens that clean blood. Perhaps only a child can present an image of the uncontaminated body, as well as soul, and there is also present the sense of a mother's fear of physical contamination. The mercuric atoms are presumably a reference to the organo-mercury compounds used in agriculture, and the well seems to be a real well. There may also, I suppose, be a reference to radioactive fall-out. Ted Hughes has a note about the poet's horror of 'the chemical poisonings of nature, the pile-up of atomic waste', in his article 'The Chronological Order of Sylvia Plath's Poems' (*Triquarterly*, no. 7, Fall 1966).

The poet loves and praises, but in no innocent or ideal glorying. This is a cold air in which the candle burns blue before yellow, nearly goes out, reminds us of the radiance in so many paintings of Mother and Child, but also of a real cold night, and of the miner's cold, his dark, his cave, his nightwork, his poisoned breathing. The intimacies and protections and colours are particular too: 'roses', 'the last of Victoriana', 'soft rugs'. The expansion moves firmly into and out of a twentieth-century world, a medieval poetry, ritual, and painting, and the earliest Christ-story, and this holds for its pains and its loving. It moves from light to dark, from love to fear. It moves beyond the images of mother-love, indeed begins outside in the first line's serious wit, 'I am a miner'. It uses—or, better, feels for—the myth of Redemption not in order to idealise the particulars but rather to revise and qualify the myth, to transplant it again cheerfully, to praise only after a long hard look at the worst. The love and faith and praise are there, wrung out and achieved against the grain, against the odds. David Holbrook is sorry that Sylvia Plath, judged from *The Bell Jar*, shows no experience of togetherness. This poem seems to embarrass his case, and it strikes me as being beyond the reach of such diagnosis or compassion. She said of the poem, in a BBC broadcast quoted by Lois Ames:[1] 'a mother

[1] 'Notes towards a Biography', *The Art of Sylvia Plath*, ed. Charles Newman (London, 1970).

nurses her baby son by candlelight and finds in him a beauty which, while it may not ward off the world's ill, does redeem her share of it'.

True, it is not typical. There are two other very loving poems of maternal feeling, 'Riddle' and 'You're', happy peals of conceits, but nothing else moves so, between these two extremities of love and pain, striking spark from such poles. 'Nick and the Candlestick' is not proffered as an instance of togetherness, but as a lucid model of the enlargement I want to discuss.

At the heart of her poetry lies the comment that she herself made about this enlargement:

> I think my poems come immediately out of the sensuous and emotional experiences I have, but I must say I cannot sympathize with these cries from the heart that are informed by nothing except a needle or a knife or whatever it is. I believe that one should be able to control and manipulate experiences, even the most terrifying—like madness, being tortured, this kind of experience—and one should be able to manipulate these experiences with an informed and intelligent mind. I think that personal experience shouldn't be a kind of shut box and mirror-looking narcissistic experience. I believe it should be generally relevant, to such things as Hiroshima and Dachau, and so on. (*Triquarterly*, no. 7, Fall 1966, p. 71)

It is interesting that Sylvia Plath uses the image of the mirror which David Holbrook also uses in that *New Society* article, called 'The 200-inch distorting mirror', in order to reject the kind of poetry he also rejects (to my mind, rightly) and which he finds (to my mind, wrongly) in Sylvia Plath.

A mere explicit statement that the poet believes personal experience of pain should not be a mirror or a shut box but should be relevant to Hiroshima and Dachau, is plainly not an answer to Holbrook. Nor would a mere listing of such references do much: the intelligent poet can after all attempt but fail to break open the shut box, may impose intellectually schematic associations with the larger world. Resnais in *Hiroshima Mon Amour* seems to be open to the charge of using the larger pain of atomic war to illuminate his personal centre, so that the movement is not that of enlargement but of diminution. Something similar seems to happen in a good many Victorian attempts to enlarge the personal problem, to combine the personal and social pain, and we may well object that the endings of *Bleak House* and *Crime and Punishment* are unsuccessful attempts to solve the large pain by the smaller reconciliation. I have spent what may seem an excessive time on 'Nick and the Candlestick' in order to establish not so much a typical feeling, but a form: the particularity and the generalisation run together in equal balance, asking questions of each other, eroding each other, unifying in true imaginative modification. I want to suggest that this is the mode of Sylvia Plath's major poetry, and that it succeeds exactly where Resnais failed. But it should be said, perhaps, that this problem of combination or enlargement works in a special way, involving artists working from experience of personal pain, depression, despair. The optimist, like Dickens and Dostoevsky, may well find it easy to join his larger pain and his smaller triumph. For the tragic artist like Sylvia Plath it is more the problem of competitive pains: how to dwell in and on the knives and needles of the personal life without shutting off the knives and needles in Biafra, Vietnam, Dachau, and Hiroshima. It is almost a problem of competing sensibilities, and the tragic artist's temptation in our time is probably to combine indecorously, like Resnais, to make the Hiroshima a metaphor for an adultery, to move from outer to inner and confirm an especially terrible shut box.

II

Before I move from 'Nick and the Candlestick' to the more terrible fusions elsewhere in *Ariel*, I want to look at some of the earlier attempts in *The Colossus* (1960). Many of the poems here show a fairly familiar and conventional tension and control. In some poems there is a narrow sensuous or social image of something painful, something dying: the dryness, unpleasant fruition, hard and yellow starlight, and difficult 'borning' of 'The Manor Garden' have nothing to say for nature; the inhuman boom and monotony of 'Night Shift' show men reduced to tend the machine; 'Hardcastle Crags' defeat the walker's energy by massive indifference and hard labour. Such poems accumulate the sense of unreward, ugliness, labour, repulsion, hostility, but each makes only its individual assertion, proffering no generalisation.

In another group of poems in this volume, there is an attempt to break up such hardness, though scarcely to redeem or transform. Such poems as 'Two Views of a Cadaver Room', 'Watercolour of Grantchester Meadows', 'The Eye-Mote' or 'Black Rook in Rainy Weather' show a darkening, rather than a darkened, vision. Affirmation is there, is valued, but is unstable. The destructive eye-mote is there for good, enlarged and confirmed as more than temporary by the move towards Oedipus, so we know that the sight cannot return, that the 'Horses fluent in the wind' are gone. In 'Black Rook in Rainy Weather' the poem sets out a belief in meaningful experience, but the belief rocks unsteadily, the experience is erratic and unguaranteed, can only bring 'A brief respite from fear/Of total neutrality'. The vigour of the meaningful moment is certainly there, 'hauling up eyelids', but in most of these poems that weigh gain against loss, there is less vigour, or a final movement towards the loss. 'Black Rook' ends with the naming of the spasmodic trick, the random rare descent, but 'The Eye-Mote' moves more characteristically away from the balance between easy fluid harmony, and the pained, blurred distorted vision, to tip the scales. We move over into blindness, guilt, loss of more than a small beauty. 'Watercolour of Grantchester Meadows' has a dark landscape, uses the spring idyll ambiguously and sharpens one point to drive it hard against our senses and sense. It creates a swimmy swoony dream of spring, water, love, in the impressionist blurring and the little nursery plate brightness, to build a bridge from the world of (superficial) sweetness to destructiveness. In 'Two Views of a Cadaver Room' the movement from death to love is deceptive: the poem allows only a tiny ambiguous space for 'the little country' where the lovers can be 'blind to the carrion army'. No redeeming corner, this, because 'foolish, Delicate' and 'not for long', stalled only 'in paint', and responding in true Brueghel disproportionateness to the earlier apparent redemption, in the first half of the poem, where after the dissection, 'He hands her the cut-out heart like a cracked heirloom'. All these poems, with the possible exception of 'Black Rook', fall out of love with the world of love, yearn for it but know what they are up against. They share a certain static quality: the pastoral term, for instance, in the Grantchester poem, is decorously but very carefully planning its own erosion, right from the start, and the poet's stance seems to be well outside the poem. Even in 'The Eye-Mote', where there is an expansion into the Oedipus myth, it is told rather than enacted: 'I dream that I am Oedipus'. Though 'the brooch-pin and the salve' effectively revise the splinter and the eye-bath, they do so by a movement of literary reference, very different from the total resonance in 'Nick' where the poem is plainly gathering its strengths and meanings, like all the best art, from conscious and unconscious assembling. The brilliant stroke of wit in 'Before the brooch-pin and the salve/

Fixed me in this parenthesis' is perhaps a limited one: the pun is dazzling in the light of the Oedipal situation, and plainly relates to all those other poems about parent-relationships. But after a little reflection one begins to wonder if *parenthesis* is quite the best word, after all, for either the Oedipal blindness or a loss of innocence. A spurt of wit remains on the superficial level. As a pun, it is not quite up to Mercutio's or Lady Macbeth's.

Ted Hughes tells us, in his *Triquarterly* piece, that the personality of Oedipus and others were important *personæ* in her life, but he is right to say that in this poem, and elsewhere, they may seem literary. It is not a matter of artificiality but of a certain thinness of feeling: the enlargement does not quite come off. Similarly, in the Grantchester poem, which strikes me perhaps as a subdued answer to Dylan Thomas's 'Sir John's Hill' (just as 'Nick' seems like a subdued answer to Hopkins's 'The Starlight Night') the movement from the human situation to the animal world seems relaxed, cool, insufficiently felt—or rather, felt to be felt in the poem. Her feelings for Greek tragedy and animal life were evidently far from thinly literary, but in some of these poems they were not yet getting sufficiently incorporated and expressed.

There are a number of poems in *Colossus*, however, where a different stance and structure achieves something much more imaginatively substantial: 'Lorelei', 'All the Dead Dears', 'Suicide Off Egg Rock', 'Full Fathom Five', 'Medallion', 'The Burnt-Out Spa' and 'Mussel Hunter at Rock Harbor' are most impressive poems of a dying fall. Each moves slowly and lucidly into a death or a longing for a death or a blessing of death. They are, if you like, perverse love-poems. Instead of working by the usual kind of enlargement, from the personal to the larger world, they attempt an empathetic drama, where a kind of death is explored, imagined, justified. If I list the last lines, a common quality in the conclusions can be my starting-point:

Stone, stone, ferry me down there. ('Lorelei') ·
Deadlocked with them, taking root as cradles rock. ('All the
    Dead Dears')
The forgetful surf creaming on those ledges. ('Suicide Off Egg
    Rock')
I would breathe water. ('Full Fathom Five')
The yardman's/Flung brick perfected his laugh. ('Medallion')

The stream that hustles us
Neither nourishes nor heals. ('The Burnt-out Spa')
. . . this relic saved/Face, to face the bald-faced sun. ('Mussel
    Hunter at Rock Harbor')

Each poem is dramatised, individualised. Each constructs a different
feeling for death. These conclusions, which all settle for death, are
earned in separate and solidly substantial ways, emotionally intense and
rationally argued, each working through a distinct human experience
which ends by wanting death.

In 'Lorelei' it is the peace of death that lures, which is why the sirens'
song and their silence are both maddening. The sense of 'maddening'
is both superficial and profound, for the listener knows that what the
sirens offer is illusion, cannot be a solicitation except in nightmare or
when 'deranged by harmony'. The images are fully responsive: 'descant
from borders/Of hebetude, from the ledge/Also of high windows' and
'Drunkenness of the great depths' and 'your ice-hearted calling'. It is
the earlier 'Sisters, your song/Bears a burden too weighty/For the
whorled ear's listening' that earns the sense of inevitability in the final
weight of 'Stone, stone'.

The same can be said of all the other poems in this group. Each makes
its individual movement to death; each is a dying. In 'All the Dead
Dears' death is repulsive, but none the less urgent for that. The dead
pull us, willy-nilly, into our graves and the three skeletons in the
Archaeological Museum are suitably and grotesquely 'unmasked' and
'dry' witnesses to life's (death's?) eating-game. The poem moves step
by step from the first instance, from the stranger-in-blood to the sense
of ancestral pull, to the father's death, through the family feasts, into a
coffin as inevitable as a cradle. The whole poem takes colour from the
first grotesque image, so that her father's death (of course a recurring
image) is seen in the right bizarre fashion: 'Where the daft father went
down/With orange duckfeet winnowing his hair', and the right,
though typically very mild (it strengthens terribly once we see through
it, though, this mildness) sense of the animal and human, and the live
and dead, overlapping. The final Gulliver image completes the grotesque line and the imagery of a trap.

The image of clarity and cleanness at the end of 'Suicide Off Egg
Rock' finishes off the man who walks away from the débris of the beach
and the muck of living—'that landscape/Of imperfections his bowels

were part of'. Each poem is a separate dying, thoroughly imagined. The apparently stoical image of the crab's face at the end of that very fine poem 'Mussel Hunter at Rock Harbor' may look like an emblem proffered to the human world by the animals, but must take on the colour of all that goes before. It is only a crab face saved, a crab death, a scrupulous rejection of symbol made at the end of a poem that has slowly forced the human being to feel itself reduced in and by the sea-beast world. The terrible 'Full Fathom Five' creates an oceanic image with human features, and the real drowned father colours the terror and makes possible a childlike plea for water rather than thick and murderous air. 'The Burnt-Out Spa' establishes, rather like 'Suicide Off Egg Rock', a rubbishy land in contrast to a pure water, and this is reinforced in the final yearning for the purified human reflection: 'It is not I, it is not I', whose sad wail is explained by all that has gone before.

These are individuated dramas of dying. The obsession is evident: the poetic flexibility, the inventive enlargements, and the self-explanatory structures show the control and the unenclosed sensibility. The actual mythological or literary symbols are part of such enlargement: the Lorelei, the drowned father in Ariel's song, the museum skeletons, Gulliver, the oriental crabface are all part of a dense formation of feeling, not tenuous-seeming annexes, like the Oedipus of 'The Eye-Mote'. It is such density that may take them to the verge of allegory, but keeps them substantially on its right side. Like much good poetry, it is tempted to be allegory, but refuses.

III

Moving to *Ariel*, the later volume, is to recognise that such inventiveness has become more powerful, and sometimes less lucid. In a poem of pain and delirium, 'Fever 103°', the wildness and fast movement of the conceits are excused by the feverishness they dramatise. They cover a wide range. They jerk from Isadora's scarves to Hiroshima ash to lemon water and chicken water; from the bizarre conceit to the simple groping, 'whatever these pink things are'; glimpses of horrors to lucidity, self-description, affectionateness, childishness: the range and the confusion establish the state of sickness. There are the other well-known poems of sickness, 'Tulips', 'In Plaster' and 'Paralytic' which dramatise individual, and different, sick states, all of them appropriately formed, in process and style. Each of these four poems is personal (which is not to say that the *persona* is not imaginary: in 'In Plaster' and 'Paralytic' it seems to be so, judging from external and internal evidence) but each is a complete and controlled drama of sick mind and body. Because it is sickness that is overtly dramatised there is no sense of an improperly won competition with the world's ills. They are brought in, by a species of decorous hallucinations. But the plainness of the act of hallucination, the lucid proffering of a febrile, convalescent, enclosed or paralysed state, allows the larger world to makes its presence properly felt. The burning in 'Fever 103°' reminds us of atomic ash, while keeping the separation clear. The plaster cast in 'In Plaster' reminds us of the other imprisonments and near-successful relationships: 'I used to think we might make a go of it together/After all, it was a kind of marriage, being so close'. I think Alun Jones is wrong to see this as an allegory about marriage:[1] these poems of sickness allow her to suggest a whole number of identifications which move towards and back from allegory. David Holbrook seems to make a different though related error in his discussion of 'Tulips': this is not a sick poem but a poem about being sick. Quite different. Of course it is a sick person who is drawn to poems about sickness, but the physical sickness makes up actual chunks of her existence, and sometimes the poems are about chilblains, cuts, influenza and appendicitis. She is drawn to sickness, mutilation, attacks, and dying, but each poem is a controlled and dynamic image with windows, not a lining of mirrors. In 'Fever' and 'In Plaster' the dramatised act of hallucination holds the personal and the social in stable and substantial mutual relationships, neither absorbing the other.

In 'Tulips' there is a slow, reluctant acceptance of the tulips, which means a slow, reluctant acceptance of a return to life. The poem dramatises a sick state, making it clear that it is sickness. The flowers are hateful, as emblems of cruel spring, as presents from the healthy world that wants her back, as suspect, like all presents. They are also emblems of irrational fear: science is brilliantly misused (as it can be in feeble and deranged states of many kinds) and phototropism and photosynthesis are used to argue the fear: the flowers really do move towards the light, do open out, do take up oxygen. The tulips are also inhabitants of the bizarre world of private irrational fantasy, even beyond the bridge of distorted science: they contrast with the whiteness of nullity and death,

---

[1] 'Necessity and Freedom: The Poetry of Robert Lowell, Sylvia Plath, and Anne Sexton', *Critical Quarterly*, vol. vii, no. 1, Spring 1965.

are like a baby, an African cat, are like her wound (a real red physical wound, stitched so as to heal, not to gape like opened tulips) and, finally, like her heart. David Holbrook's analysis of this poem seems to stop short of the transforming end, which opens up the poem. The poem, like the tulips, has really been opening from the beginning, but all is not plain until the end, as in 'Nick'. Holbrook says, 'The tulips, as emissaries of love, seem to threaten her with emptying of the identity: "the vivid tulips eat my oxygen" ', but the tulips win, and that is the point. It is a painful victory for life. We move from the verge of hallucination, which can hear them as noisy, or see them as like dangerous animals, to a proper rationality, which accepts recovery. The poem hinges on this paradox: while most scientific, it is most deranged; while most surreal, it is most healthy:

> And I am aware of my heart: it opens and closes
> Its bowl of red blooms out of sheer love of me.
> The water I taste is warm and salt, like the sea,
> And comes from a country far away as health.

It is the country she has to return to, reluctant though she is: the identification of the breathing, opened, red, springlike tulips with her heart makes this plain. She wanted death, certainly, as one may want it in illness or, moving back from the poem to the other poems and to her real death, as she wanted it in life. But the poem enacts the movement from the peace and purity of anaesthesia and feebleness to the calls of life. Once more, the controlled conceits and the movement from one state to another create expansion. The poem opens out to our experience of sickness and health, to the overwhelming demands of love, which we sometimes have to meet. The symbolism of present-giving and spring-flowers makes a bridge from a personal death-longing to common experience: something very similar can be found in the short poem 'Poppies in October' which uses a similar symbolism and situation for a different conclusion and feeling; and in the magnificent Bee poems, where the solid facts and documentations of beekeeping act as a symbolic base for irrational and frightening fantasy *and* as a bridge into the everyday and ordinary explanations and existences.

The concept of explicit hallucination seems useful. In the Bee poems we move away from the poetry of sickness to another kind of rejected allegory. These poems stress technical mysteries. The craft and ritual of bee-keeping are described with a Kafkaesque suggestiveness, and can take off into a larger terror and come back after all into the common and solid world. In 'The Bee Meeting', her lack of protective clothing, her feeling of being an outsider, then an initiate, the account of the disguised villagers and the final removal of disguise, the queenbee, the spiky gorse, the box—all are literal facts which suggest paranoic images but remain literal facts. The poem constantly moves between the two poles of actuality and symbolic dimension, right up to and including the end. A related poem, 'The Arrival of the Bee Box', works in the same way, but instead of suggesting paranoiac fear and victimisation, puts the beekeeper into an unstable allegorical God-position. The casual slangy 'but my god' unobtrusively works towards the religious enlargement:

> I am no source of honey
> So why should they turn on me?
> Tomorrow I will be sweet God, I will set them free.

> The box is only temporary.

After the suggestiveness comes the last line, belonging more to the literal beekeeping facts, but pulled at least briefly into the symbolic orbit. These are poems of fear, a fear which seems mysterious, too large for its occasion. They allow for a sinister question to raise itself, between the interpretation and the substance. The enlargement which is inseparable from this derangement is morally vital and viable: these poems are about power and fear, killing and living, and the ordinariness and the factual detail work both to reassure us and to establish that most sinister of fears, the fear of the familiar world. Perhaps the most powerful Bee poem comes in the New York edition of *Ariel*, 'The Swarm' (also printed in *Winter Trees*). Here the enlargement is total and constant, for the poem equates the destruction of the swarm with a Napoleonic attack, and presents a familiar argument for offensive action: 'They would have killed *me*'. It presents two objective correlatives, the bees and Napoleon, in an unfailing grim humour

> Stings big as drawing pins!
> It seems bees have a notion of honour,
> A black, intractable mind.
> Napoleon is pleased, he is pleased with everything.
> O Europe! O ton of honey!

The humour comes out of the very act of derangement: imagine comparing this with that, just imagine. It depends on the same kind of rationally alert intelligence that controls 'Fever 103°'.

It is present in the great *Ariel* poems: 'Lady Lazarus', 'Daddy',[1] 'Death & Co.', 'A Birthday Present' and 'The Applicant', which are very outgoing, very deranged, very enlarged. In 'Lady Lazarus' the *persona* is split, and deranged. The split allows the poem to peel off the personal, to impersonate suicidal feeling and generalise it. It is a skill, it is a show, something to look at. The poem seems to be admitting the exhibitionism of suicide (and death-poetry?) as well as the voyeurism of spectators (and readers?). It is also a foul resurrection, stinking of death. This image allows her to horrify us, to complain of being revived, to attack God and confuse him with a doctor, any doctor (bringing round a suicide) and a Doktor in a concentration camp, experimenting in life and death. It moves from Herr Doktor to Herr Enemy and to miraclemakers, scientists, the torturer who may be a scientist, to Christ, Herr God, and Herr Lucifer (the last two after all collaborated in experiments on Adam, Eve, and Job). They poke and nose around in the ashes, and this is the last indignity, forcing the final threat: 'I eat men like air'. It is a threat that can intelligibly be made by martyred victims (she has red hair, is Jewish), by phoenixes, by fire, by women. The fusion and dispersal, once more rational and irrational, makes the pattern of controlled derangement, creating not one mirror but a hall of mirrors, all differently distorting, and revealing many horrors. Such complexity of reference, such enactment of desperation, hysteria and hate, permits at times the utterly bare cry, like the endearment in 'Nick': 'I turn and burn'. Again, the range of tone is considerable. There is the dry irony, only capable of life in such surroundings of hysteria: 'Do not think I underestimate your great concern', and the slangy humour, 'I guess you could say I've a call', which, like the communion tablet in 'Tulips' is an anti-religious joke, not a solemn allusion, though you do not see the joke unless you feel the solemnity. There is the sensuous particularity, extremely unpleasant. It is tactual, visual and olfactory: 'Pick the worms off me like sticky pearls', 'full set of teeth' and 'sour breath'. The sheer active hostility of the poem works through the constant shift from one mode to another, one tone to

---

[1] A. Alvarez is particularly good on this poem, 'Sylvia Plath', *Triquarterly*, no. 7, Fall 1966, reproduced in *Beyond All This Fiddle* (London, 1968).

another, one *persona* to another. It races violently and spasmodically towards the climax.

This kind of structural derangement of structure, which allows for collision, a complex expansion, and a turn in several directions, sometimes becomes very surrealist in dislocation. It fragments into opaque parts, as in that most baffling poem, 'The Couriers', and in 'The Applicant'. We might be tempted to see the enlargement in 'The Applicant' as an allegory of marriage, relationship, dependence, were if not for the violent twist with which the poem shuffles off such suggestions:

> First, are you our sort of a person?
> Do you wear
> A glass eye, false teeth or a crutch,
> A brace or a hook,
> Rubber breasts or a rubber crotch,
>
> Stitches to show something's missing? No, no? Then
> How can we give you a thing?
> Stop crying.
> Open your hand.
> Empty? Empty. Here is a hand
>
> To fill it and willing
> To bring teacups and roll away headaches
> And do whatever you tell it.
> Will you marry it?
> It is guaranteed
>
> To thumb shut your eyes at the end
> And dissolve of sorrow.
> We make new stock from the salt.
> I notice you are stark naked.
> How about this suit—
>
> Black and stiff, but not a bad fit.
> Will you marry it?
> It is waterproof, shatterproof, proof
> Against fire and bombs through the roof.
> Believe me, they'll bury you in it.

The hand to fill the empty hand and shut the eyes, or (later) the naked doll that can sew, cook, talk, move towards this allegory, but the black stiff suit 'waterproof, shatterproof' in which 'they'll bury you' moves away towards any kind of panacea or protection. What holds the poem together, controlling such opacities of derangement, is the violent statement of deficiency hurled out in the first stanza, and the whole violent imitation of the language of salesmanship, the brisk patter of question, observation, suggestion and recommendation. The enlargement works not just through the ill-assembled fragments—hand, suit, and in the later stanzas, doll—but through the satirised speech, which relates needs, deficiencies, dependence and stupid panaceas to the larger world. Life (or love) speaks in the cheap-jack voice, as well it may, considering what it may seem to have to offer. This is an applicant not just for relationship, for marriage, for love, for healing, but for life and death.

This brilliant linguistic impersonation works more generally in these poems, as a source of black humour, as satiric enlargement, as a link with ordinariness, as unselfpitying speech. It is present in small doses but with large effect in the massive, rushing, terrible poem, 'Getting There'. Here the death train is also the painful dying, the dragging life, also wars, machines, labour. The poem questions, and the questions stagger: 'How far is it? How far is it now?' It dwells painfully and slowly in the present tense: 'I am dragging my body . . . And now detonations . . . The train is dragging itself'. Its derangements present animals and machines in a mangling confusion: the interior of the wheels is 'a gorilla interior', the wheels eat, the machines are brains and muzzles, the train breathes, has teeth, drags and screams like an animal. There is a painful sense of the body's involvement in the machine, the body made to be a wheel. The image creates an entanglement, involves what Sartre calls the 'dilapidation' of surrealism. There is the horror of a hybrid monster, a surrealist crossing of animal with machine. The rational arguments and logical connections are frightening in their precision. The wheel and the gorilla's face can be confused into one image, big, round, dark, powerful. Krupp's 'brains' is almost literally correct. The train noise can sound like a human scream, the front of a train can look like a face.

The method of combination as well as the content, as in all good poetry, generates the passions. The sense of strain, of hallucination, of doing violence to the human imagery is a consequence of the derangements. The rational excuses simply play into the hands of such sense of strain, by making it work visually, bringing it close, giving it substance and connection with the real European world. The movement is a double one, it creates a trope and a form for unbearable pain, and intolerable need for release. It enlarges the personal horror and suggests a social context and interpretation, in Krupp, in the train, in Russia, in the marvellously true and fatigued 'some war or other', in the nurses, men, hospital, in Adam's side and the woman's body 'Mourned by religious figures, by garlanded children'. And finally, in Lethe. Its end and climax is as good as that in 'Nick':

> And I, stepping from this skin
> Of old bandages, boredoms, old faces

> Step to you from the black car of Lethe,
> Pure as a baby.

There is the naked appearance of the myth new-made, the feeling that Lethe has had to wait till now to be truly explained, as the Nativity had to wait for 'Nick'. After such pain of living and dying, after so many bewildered identifications, after such pressure and grotesque confusion, we must step right out of the skin. And when we do, the action reflects back, and the body seems to have been the train. This adds another extension of the derangement of human, animal, and mechanical. After this, only Lethe. The poem then begins to look like a nightmare of dying, the beginning of forgetting, the lurching derangements working as they do in dreams.

Once more, the expansion permits the naked cry. This happens more quietly and sadly in 'The Moon and the Yew Tree' where the movement outward is against the Christian myth, but works so as to generalise, to show the active seeking mind in the exercise of knowledge and comparison. This movement explains, permits, and holds up the bare dreadful admission, 'I simply cannot see where there is to get to'. The feeling throughout is one of deep and tried depression. The moon is no light, no door:

> It is a face in its own right,
> White as a knuckle and terribly upset.

The oddity and childishness of the funny little analogy, and the simple bare statement, 'terribly upset' all contribute to the tiredness. So does the science of 'drags the sea after it like a dark crime' and the conceit 'the O-gape of complete despair', which have a slight archness and flickering humour, like someone very tired and wretched who tries a smile. Nature is all too simply interpreted, coloured by 'the light of the mind', is cold, planetary, black, blue. The moon is quite separate from the consolations of religion, though there are echoes of other myths which emphasise this, of Hecate and witchcraft, as in 'The Disquieting Muses'. Such sinister suggestions, like the remote and decorative images of the saints, 'all blue,/Floating on their delicate feet over the cold pews,/Their hands and faces stiff with holiness' are made in a matter-of-fact, slightly arch way. These are Stanley Spencer-like visions, made in a childish, tired voice: 'The moon is my mother. She is not sweet like Mary./Her blue garments unloose small bats and owls'. The very quietness, compared with her more violent poems of fear, has its own stamp of acceptance. The several bald statements in the poem belong to the quiet tired prevailing tone: 'How I would like to believe in tenderness' and 'the message of the yew tree is blackness—blackness and silence'.

This poem of deep depression still enlarges, still knows about the larger world, still tries a tired but personal humour:

> Eight great tongues affirming the Resurrection.
> At the end, they soberly bong out their names.

The poem's empathy is powerful, but it is perhaps most powerful when it is dropped. The end returns to the explicit act of interpretation —what do the moon and the yew tree mean?—of the beginning. The poem moves heavily into the meditation, then out of it. There has been an attempt at enlargement, but the colours here are the colours of the mind, and the attempts at mythical explanation or extension all fail. It seems like a poem about making the effort to write out of depression, where the act of enlargement is difficult, the distance that can be covered is short.

In 'A Birthday Present' the same process shapes a different passion. The enlargement in this poem is again a movement towards Christian myth, this time a perverted annunciation. The poem longs for release, like so many others, but in its individual mood. This time she pleads and reasons carefully, patiently, with humility, is willing to take a long time over it. The pace of her poems varies tremendously, and while 'Daddy', 'Lady Lazarus' and 'Getting There' move with sickening speed, 'A Birthday Present' is appallingly slow. Its slowness is right for its patience and its feeling of painful burden. It is created by the pleas,

'Let it not . . . Let it not', and the repetitions which here put the brakes on, though in other poems they can act as accelerators. Its questioning slows up, and so does its vagueness, and its unwillingness to argue endlessly—or almost endlessly. The humilities are piteously dramatised: 'I would not mind . . . I do not want much of a present . . . Can you not . . . If you only knew . . . only you can give it to me . . . Let it not'. There is the childishness, horrifying in the solemn pleasure of 'there would be a birthday'. From time to time there is the full, adult, knowing, reasoning voice, that can diagnose, 'I know why you will not'; reassure, 'Do not be afraid'; and be ironic, 'O adding machine/Is it impossible for you to let something go and have it whole?/Must you stamp each piece in purple . . .'

It is not surprising that Sylvia Plath felt constrained to speak these late poems: they are dramatised, voiced, often opaque but always personalised. Their enlargements are made within the personal voice: groping for the resemblance to some war, some annunciation, some relationship, some institution, some Gothic shape, some prayer, some faith. Even where there is a movement towards the larger world, as in 'The Moon and the Yew Tree' or 'A Birthday Present', it has a self-consciousness, a deployment of knowledge, a reasoning, a sense of human justice, that keeps it from being sick or private. The woman who measures the flour and cuts off the surplus, adhering 'to rules, to rules, to rules', and the mind that sees the shortcomings of adding-machines is a *persona* resisting narcissism and closure, right to the death.

Ronald Laing is involved in that cult of schizophrenia which has encouraged both an excessive admiration and an excessive rejection of a clinically limited poetry of derangement. I believe that Sylvia Plath's poetry is not so limited, but I should nevertheless like to remember Laing's comment that few books in our time are forgiveable, and to suggest that *The Colossus* and *Ariel* are amongst those few.

Index

This index is restricted to persons referred to by name or by work in the text and to anonymous works. Italic page numbers indicate substantial discussion.